# Joe the Salamander

## About This Book

*Joe the Salamander* is an unforgettable book. It is a story of one man's journey of survival in a world that is extremely difficult to navigate when you are "not like everyone else". Strong female characters like Millie, Joe's mother, and his mentor Laura accepted him unconditionally for all of his uniqueness. It is with their unconditional love, support and understanding that Joe went from being alone to having a life second to none. This is an uplifting and heartfelt story.

—**Carol Gillis**, MS ABA, BCBA, LABA Senior Director of Autism Services at The Edinburg Center in Bedford MA

Gager both invokes psychological insight and mocks its blindness. He imagines an autistic child's coming of age, both through and outside the child's eyes. From infancy, Joe "thinks" articulately, but rarely speaks, and his understanding of the world of *Not Me* is wry and sensitive, somewhat like Faulkner's Benjy's. The reader accepts Joe's early *Superman* obsession, which translates into a defensive fantasy of having "powers"; but the novel goes beyond *tour de force* to sheer inspiration as it follows Joe, his parents, a friendly nurse, and many other characters though his stages to maturity—and then delivers a tragic complication with 9/11. Joe's parents have been vacationing in New York, and Joe sees them in a tv replay: "There his father was, hanging on the edge of a window. He was small on the screen in his blue suit, and holding onto him was his mother....None of them could fly, and no one could be saved."

—**DeWitt Henry**, author of *Endings and Beginnings: Family Essays*

I have worked on complicated television projects like *The Assassination of Gianni Versace*, where how we choose to tell the story can be as risky as the story we are trying to tell. It can either go well or.... But, in my opinion, Timothy Gager has knocked *Joe the Salamander* out of the park, pulling us into the mind of a non-verbal infant, and then pulling us through his life as witnesses to his confusion and pain. The entire book unfolds with cinematic grace, leaving me wanting more. I'd love to see this on a screen, or on my desk as a screenplay soon.

—**Korey Pollard**, Assistant Director/Producer, *What Remains, The Assassination of Gianni Versace, House M.D., Deadwood, Clear and Present Danger, Monk*

# Joe the Salamander

by

## Timothy Gager

*Golden Antelope Press*
715 E. McPherson
Kirksville, Missouri 63501
2022

ISBN:      9781952232695

Library of Congress Control Number: 2022932989

Published by:
Golden Antelope Press
715 E. McPherson
Kirksville, Missouri 63501

Available at:
Golden Antelope Press
715 E. McPherson
Kirksville, Missouri, 63501
Phone: (660) 665-0273
http://www.goldenantelope.com
Email: ndelmoni@gmail.com

# Dedication

*For my siblings, their families, my dad, and SPG.*

*For all those who are challenged daily by anything physical, mental, or emotional. May the world be kind.*

*For those we have lost and those who live 24-7 a day, an hour, a minute at a time, don't waste life's time. You never know what the next second brings.*

-TG

*The word "Salamander" is derived from an old Arab/Persian word meaning "lives in fire," stemming from an old belief, false of course, that the salamander could walk through fire and remain unharmed.*

\* \* \*

*"A trapped person will eventually jump from the window of a burning high-rise. Make no mistake about people who leap from burning windows. Their terror of falling from a great height is still just as great as it would be for you or me standing speculatively at the same window just checking out the view; i.e. the fear of falling remains a constant. The variable here is the other terror, the fire's flames: when the flames get close enough, falling to death becomes the slightly less terrible of two terrors. It's not desiring the fall; it's terror of the flames. And yet nobody down on the sidewalk, looking up and yelling 'Don't!' and 'Hang on!', can understand the jump. Not really. You'd have to have personally been trapped and felt flames to really understand a terror way beyond falling."*

*-David Foster Wallace*

# Adrian's Prologue

Multiply your age times 365, then add the days from your last birthday until today, and those are the exact odds that the next day will be worse than the worst day of your life. Here was mine: I was at the dining room table working on advanced high school algebra when the police came. I was only 12 at the time. Numbers were my friends. My parents were dead, the police said, and then, to gather my stuff.

I never spoke much to the first foster parents. If I focused on my real parents, I imagined the foster ones might feel slighted. They might not keep me. It was awkward, because all I felt was sad. They bought me new glasses. They bought white button down shirts. Shoes. Books. Toothpaste. *Everything is temporary*, the man from the foster care agency said.

The next three sets of parents were permanent placements. *They didn't work out*, said the same man, who said the exact same thing every time he picked me up from a failed pairing. *No bond was formed.*

I shrugged at him. I never spoke to the man about the times I received black eyes and had my glasses broken. I was moved all over Arizona in the next six years. Not exactly a tour. I couldn't wait to get out on my own.

My final foster parents asked me to plant grass in the desert. The father's name was Walter. I never called him dad. The mother's name I never learned. I called her Mrs. Walter, just to feel I had something on them. I dug the dirt for hours. The seeds didn't take all that much. I knew nothing about growth. The grass that started looked like the random hairs on the top of Walter's head. I watered the yard looking for a miracle. In those days, I pushed my glasses up often because of the sweat, or picked them off the ground after they were slapped off my face. I was a good worker but the goal of work is to produce.

Walter told me this while I was pressing a tissue against my puffed out lip.

At Boston University, when I tell Millie this, in her high-rise dormitory on Commonwealth Avenue, she starts to cry. She gives me the confidence to talk and be heard, so she has a role in all this. I decide right there that she is the only one I'll ever tell my story to. I was invited to this dormitory tower last night because I hated the cold, but, really, she wanted me to stay. It's too cold in Boston, but Millie's dorm room is as warm as the sun in Tempe. When Millie returns from composing herself, I say, "It is too late for any more new parents, and since I'm over eighteen, I'm legally on my own." Millie looks baffled, pauses enough for me to fill the silence. "Look," I say, "I've worked hard to get here, applying on my own; and I selected the one as far away as possible from where I lived, on a full scholarship. This is the reason we met. I did this all myself. I plan to go back to Arizona as soon as I graduate, and I hope you come with me. It's warm, and it's what I'm used to." This is what I tell her. I'm not sure if I'm saying the right things.

# Part I

# Chapter One

Joe was born into the searing bright light, and when the doctor slapped him, he didn't cry or do much of anything. When he slapped him again, and Joe still did not cry, the delivery team went ahead and ran all the tests for newborns. Joe had a perfectly logical reason to not cry, but no one would ever know it.

Joe's coloring was perfect, a bright healthy red, and he was breathing well enough, even with a small amount of amniotic fluid in his lungs. All combined, the doctors were not worried about his well-being. His APGAR scale rating was a six, recording two points each for the appearance, pulse, and respiration categories, but it had zeros in the categories for grimace and activity. Joe was measured to have zero reaction to outside stimulus. As his mother, Millie, cradled him in the hospital bed, Joe lay there like a lump, almost afraid to ask for anything, as if a newborn would need anything more than a cuddle or perhaps the dampening of lights, sounds, or chaos.

Joe's father, Adrian Gamut, currently was nowhere to be found. It wasn't because he was an absentee father, or avoiding the happenings of Joe's birth, but rather because he was completely overwhelmed. So instead, he passed out candy cigars to strangers on the street. There was a certain beauty in such a basic interaction: *here have a cigar made from candy, and you will never have to see me again.* Much less beautiful was that right before Adrian passed out a cigar, he had to push his inexpensive glasses back up against the bridge of his nose, even more than he usually did. Sweat will do that.

Millie wasn't concerned with Adrian's disappearance. She knew he was odd, unable to properly read social cues, logical, inflexible, and miserably anxious most of the time. He was a freak, but he was her freak. His parents had died in a car accident when he was twelve, and because of this, she knew, he would never leave her. He'd even said, *when we go, we must go at the same time.*

Millie knew her husband was the kind of person who would simmer in an emotion until the affect dissipated, almost the way that the horn of an approaching train builds in sound, peaks into a crescendo, and then disappears into thin air. It was like a bell curve, and Adrian, like all good accountants, understood how measurements ebbed and flowed. During Millie's pregnancy, he had earned her trust about being a hands-on parent, something that his foster care placements had tended to be clueless about.

Meanwhile, Joe, at this point, was making no sound at all. *He is going to be a good baby*, Millie thought, *he is going to be no trouble at all.* The nursing staff was very troubled though.

"Isn't he a darling?" was all they'd say, before moving on to the next patient in the maternity ward, where their babies were all said to be beautiful, gorgeous, and handsome. There were other darlings too, all within Millie's earshot, because no matter how unique a baby is, there are only so many adjectives one could think up during a twelve hour shift. Out of Millie's hearing, the words, *possibly brain damaged*, had been spoken between some of them.

But Millie didn't know that. She only knew that every baby couldn't be darling, beautiful, gorgeous, and handsome, just like adults couldn't all be good things. Even if someone called her beautiful, she would shape the words into the reality of her understanding. She knew she was only just tall enough, or attractive enough, to get by. She knew she blended in. This is why Millie was cynical when it came to compliments. She knew the nurses were just doing their jobs, and Joe wasn't darling at all. The nurses obviously had to say positive things, the same way car salesmen would trumpet the only outstanding quality of a shitty car. *The engine might not feel powerful, but it gets excellent gas mileage.* She thought the nurses were trained to be this way, or rather, wouldn't have jobs if they told the honest truth. Maybe Joe was the opposite of *darling*, but she thought he was just about perfect anyhow, so what did their opinions matter? All of these thoughts, after just having given birth, exhausted her, and she was asleep immediately after closing her eyes, and then immediately after she was assigned a hospital room.

# Chapter Two

Adrian was exhausted too. He had been racing around the Banner Good Samaritan Hospital campus handing out blue and pink candy cigars. After, he had roamed an additional two miles to the innovative new Phoenix Children's Hospital, which smelled fresh, new, and not at all like the antiseptic smell of illness the older hospitals had. It didn't matter to him that the cigars he held were both pink and blue. Adrian had bought boxes for both possibilities of gender, as he had not wanted to know the sex in advance. When he distributed the pink ones, he just yelled, "It's a Boy! Sorry!" It also didn't matter to him that he was doing this at Phoenix Children's Hospital, which mostly served children who were currently sick; he was beside himself with joy. If there was any push back from parents, worried about their own children and not wishing to celebrate with him, he'd just say the "Sorry," part.

Adrian was non-athletic, not in the best shape for someone in his twenties, so running around in the heat at 3:30 p.m. made him feel sick too. Contrary to the myth of high noon, Phoenix was its hottest between 3:00 and 4:00 p.m. Also, as humidity crept in during the summer, the "dry heat" was another myth busted.

Before they moved there he used to tell Millie, "It gets so hot in Phoenix that you can fry an egg on the sidewalk." That also wasn't true. He'd tried it as a kid, and it hadn't worked. He researched, and according to a cookbook owned by one of his foster mothers, the frying pan needed to be heated to 158 degrees, and the sidewalks in Arizona never reached that.

Adrian's lungs burned, and his sweat drenched his shirt. He had to constantly push the bridge of his glasses against his nose, or they might slide off and break. He'd been to the optometrist for an adjustment, but after a few hours his glasses would slip down again, so he kept making more appointments to have them tightened again. Logically an optometrist should be able to find a solution for this problem.

Adrian was about finished. He had just run the equivalent of a 5K around the areas neighboring the two hospitals. He was worn out and decided to walk, instead of run, back to Banner Good Samaritan Hospital. He was still breathing hard, his head bowed, glasses barely hanging on his face, while clutching two cigars in each hand, two blue, and two pink. On Thomas Road, a young couple nearby noticed his distressed state. From the outside they looked like typical Arizonians, but as they walked closer to Adrian, they appeared to have been up all night, and all of the morning partying. She had a limp, but her winged-back blonde hair was cemented and unmoved by her gait. She wore enough makeup to cover three people, and her orange tee-shirt had the sleeves cut off, producing an open vent that allowed Adrian to inhale some of the sour smell which wafted from under her arms.

"Are you okay?" the woman asked, pulling on a sleeve of the extra-large, well worn, Phoenix Suns tee-shirt. Adrian huffed out a quick "Yes," as his glasses fell to the ground. The woman bent down, and retrieved them for him. It was from this perspective she noticed the cigars in his hand.

"Congratulations! Did you have quadruplets?"

Adrian was light-headed and mentally fatigued. It had taken a lot out of him extending himself to strangers at the hospitals. Now that he had stopped his expedition, he longed for people he knew to surround him and Millie in their hospital room at Banner. He was tired of speaking to strangers. He was hoping this interaction would be quick and easy.

"Yes," he breathed.

"Oh, that's wonderful," the woman said. "A boy and a girl. Can we have a cigar? How about a blue one for me and a pink one for Bobby, there?" Bobby looked like he needed something to get his saliva up and running. Adrian hoped the guy wouldn't collapse, fearing even worse, that he would have to resuscitate him if he collapsed, because Adrian felt like collapsing himself.

"Yes," Adrian repeated.

He handed her the pink one. "No. No. Bobby's over there."

"Yes."

"Give me the blue one."

"Yes."

"Are you sure, you're okay?"

"Yes."

"You're not looking too well."

"Yes." The air was so hot that Adrian's words squeaked out of him.

"You sure you're okay?" she asked, "Because, The Good Sam is right over there," using the hospital's common nickname.

"Yes."

"Okay, then. Congratulations, and thanks for the cigars."

Again, he said, "Yes," as if it was the only word possible.

\* \* \*

Within ten minutes of getting back to the newly assigned room, Adrian was asleep in the beige hospital lounge chair. Millie, also sleeping, was breathing gently, wearing a slight smile. Millie's teeth were slightly crooked, but not crooked enough to have required braces as a teenager. Her dark hair remained stringy from the delivery; the sweat had visibly dried to salt on her forehead. It made her look older, although her natural maturity meant that she was often seen as years older than she was. Her body was soft in places women's bodies become around the time they give birth. Baby Joe was curled on the mattress, his head against the space where Millie's arm met the sheet. He was not asleep. He was quiet, comfortably wrapped in the hospital's white blanket adorned with pink and aqua colored stripes.

When the nurses checked in, both Adrian and Millie were still sleeping, so they took infant Joe to run their own unofficial tests on him. It was then that Joe felt heaviness in his diaphragm. His shallow breaths quickened. The nurse quickly spoke to Joe in a hushed tone.

"No, honey, it's alright. It's alright," she said, but in a way that tiny Joe misunderstood, in context, feeling he was doing something wrong. Joe calmed quickly in the nurse's arms. What they didn't know, as there was no way they could have, was that this was the first time Joe had attempted to both please people, and to disappear from the world. What they did know was a growing concern, causing various emergency meetings, about a baby born that wouldn't cry.

# Chapter Three

Adrian awoke with a mix of adrenaline and anxiety, his glasses helicoptering off his face. Where was Joe? Where was his son? Had he been stolen? What would he and Millie do if Joe disappeared? He knew Millie would handle it in a way that would be as level-headed and calm, given the situation, as possible. He, on the other hand, although logical, would probably do something he might regret–a panic, or overreaction.

He bolted into the hallway, stopped, then lurched up to the nurses' station, which was directly in front of him. He stood there, but couldn't seem to get any words out—almost as if he had forgotten how to form speech.

"Mr. Gamut," a young nurse positioned dead-center at the station said. She clutched a gold cross on the chain around her neck and pulled it back and forth. "Don't worry, he's in the nursery now. That way, you and your wife can get some rest. There won't be much opportunity for that pretty soon, once you get home. Not that Joe would be a bother as he's such a quiet boy—he just looks around, taking things in. It's pretty perfect, if you ask me. I'm Nurse Wellin, but please, call me Laura." Laura was not worried by Joe's lack of crying. On the contrary, she thought he was amazing, and super evolved.

"Oh, thank you, Laura Wellin," he answered, the words suddenly and freely forming as she had put him at ease.

"Just Laura, and relax. Your son is no problem for us," Laura said, shaking her long, straight blonde hair back over her shoulder. "Maybe this is a first time experience for you, but we do this all the time."

Adrian, for once, knew exactly what was meant, though often he had trouble understanding the intent of conversation. As often with information, which could be nuanced, the meaning and interpretation might get distorted. In fact, this interaction could have sounded accusatory to him, as if he weren't capable of being a father. Yet Adrian knew that Laura was kind and spoke in calm, caring tones, so he recognized that instead of being accused of something terrible, he was being reassured. Thank God for the obviousness of this, as things often seemed impossible for him to figure out. In fact, he cataloged all misunderstood exchanges or social blunders, and he saved them in his brain as regretful mistakes he would try to avoid. It was the long mental list he had begun, at age twelve, while in foster care. Also, what about her saying, *we do this all the time,* as she looked so young? There was a disconnect for Adrian regarding *all the time.* He could not have known that Laura had graduated from her nursing program early, nor could he tell that she was just a couple of years younger than his wife. Back when he was twelve, too many misunderstood social cues would put Adrian on the road to a new residence, with new foster parents, time and time again. He had learned to be cautious.

# Chapter Four

It had been about a week and Joe had not cried. He was eating, and drinking enough formula, so the doctors and nurses at Banner Good Samaritan Maternity Ward didn't worry about his physical health. They did worry about the peculiarity of his lack of crying, and there were mixed views about whether it was a medical abnormality or whether perhaps Joe was some sort of miracle baby. They ruled out lack of vocal cords because Joe was uttering some low noises. Besides, if he were able to cry without having vocal cords, there certainly would be visual signs he was doing so—perhaps looking like a muted television set. Because of this, Joe had been kept in the hospital longer than the typical 48 hours, and they'd diagnosed his specific "health problem" as some form of Familial Dysautonomia.

Without the audio cue of crying, Laura would independently bring Joe to his mother for feedings, on schedule, eight times per day. Laura had volunteered to be the point nurse for the Gamut baby, as she was in the miracle baby camp. Although she had been taught not to form bonds or have favorites, Joe Gamut fascinated her. The more days that went by without crying, the more magical it seemed. Laura was attracted to things like that, such as the Banner Good Samaritan Hospital's telling nickname, The Good Sam. It had made her want to become a nurse at a good place.

Millie Gamut was incredibly laid back for a first-time parent. Most first-timers would treat their newborn like a yo-yo. *Bring them in from the nursery. Take them back out. Are they hungry? Why won't they breastfeed? Why are they crying?* This was the standard fare for most new parents. Many a first-time mother unsuccessfully attempted to breastfeed before her milk came in, or suffered from chapped nipples, then tried to dominate the time of the lactation specialist. Laura could easily answer all the questions or help with lactation issues, but young Laura was learning through experience to leave things for the new mother to discover on her own.

Then there were the mothers who quickly discovered, during this time, that the more time their little darlings spent in the nursery, the better it was for them. They all knew it was the calm before the storm, as suddenly they would be home and it would be a full-time job. Laura felt that these mothers treated their stay at The Good Sam as if it were a hotel with a nanny service. Then the fathers would fall into place, taking naps in the room with the mother or flipping through the hospital's television channels. Often, Laura wondered what life would be like to sleep all day, to inquire briefly how things were around her responsibilities, and then request a can of pineapple juice. Millie Gamut was something different. Millie didn't seem like a first-time mother. She acted as if she were coming in for her second, third, or fourth time. Laura liked her immediately. She envied Millie's poise and her ability to be herself, even after delivering a child into the world. Millie even said that Joe's lack of crying was, *just the way he is and he is going to be fine*, which Laura thought was a perfect stress free way of looking at it. The father, Adrian, didn't speak negatively on that issue, but that seemed more because he was, in general, oblivious and avoidant of people, places, and things. Adrian paced The Good Sam's floors a lot.

The Nurse Director of Maternity Services, Mary Mullray, wasn't as laid back as Millie or as avoidant as Adrian. Mary was direct, and to the point, and ruled by the book. She knew, by the book, that a baby who had a measured abnormality must be fixed as much as medically possible. She was adamant to her staff about this, in her not so warm and fuzzy way. Mary Mullray checked the doctor's and nurse's notes constantly for any news of Joe crying. When there wasn't any, she reminded the team that they had better not miss anything medically before Joe was sent home, and she was much in favor of Joe going home as soon as possible–but only after he proved he could cry. Joe was costing the hospital money, but legally it was safer for them to keep him. Mary Mullray wanted to save money without taking legal risks. So she devised a plan, one which wasn't based on any book, regulation, or formal assessment. It was medically necessary, she concluded, and thus could be done without questions.

On the day of Joe's one week birthday, Mary Mullray informed

Laura that they would be going in a new direction. It was something that hadn't been tried in any hospital before, and it would be so groundbreaking that neither Adrian nor Millie would be allowed in the room for the procedure. Also, it needed to be done today. Laura knew that when Mary Mullray requested that you do something, you'd better respond like it's coming from the mouth of God or else there would be consequences. She also knew that Mary Mullray's overzealous requests were often power plays. The bottom line was that Laura was being ordered by God, if God were a monster—to force a baby to cry. It was an order which caused her to run to the bathroom and burst into tears.

# Chapter Five

Laura was usually overly gracious at taking orders. She was a people pleaser who honestly believed that the world would be a kinder, better place if everyone would try to people please a little bit more. She could please her entire hospital team, if she was compliant to Mary Mullray's order, but how would she please baby Joe, who would not cry? And use compassion to get the desired result? She quickly did a Ben Franklin pros-and-cons table in her head, somehing she often did to help her make difficult decisions.

Pros:

1. ) If there were something medically wrong besides his inability to cry, I could help fix it.
2. ) If I could make Joe cry after this large amount of time, and I was the one who successfully helped him to do so, I could be nationally news worthy.
3. ) If I simply followed orders, I would be in the forefront of my team, increasing my job status because I was doing what no one else wanted to do. Who wants to make a baby cry?
4. ) Afterward, I would get to be the first person to comfort Joe.
5. ) It is my job to obey Mary Mullray.

Cons:

1. ) I might cause undue distress to an infant, violating the Hippocratic Oath.
2. ) I could accidentally cause another injury and be in the national news.
3. ) I could get fired.
4. ) Baby Joe may never stop crying, once I start him.

5. ) It is my job to obey Mary Mullray.

Laura walked two laps around the maternity floor to sort out her decision. Her shoes squeaked as she rounded turn three of lap one, which distracted her from her inner debate. In her head, she had already prepared to tell Mary Mullray, *I don't feel comfortable doing this.* Then she thought, *Mercy, I need to wear different shoes.*

Laura continued her walk, and concluded that even with the cons, she was the one best suited for this assignment, and it should not be left to anyone else. She was more likely to achieve an outcome from the pros list, while her co-workers might be capable of something appearing on the cons list. Also helping her decide was passing the anxious-looking Adrian, also pacing the floor.

Laura never finished the second lap, but instead veered into the nursery, the way a race car enters the pit area. Two of her co-workers sat on rocking chairs giving babies bottles. Joe lay on his back, in a bassinet, looking up, not smiling, not crying, not doing much of anything. She looked at him sadly and reached down to pull him up. She tightened the blanket around him, so it was snug, so it felt like a second skin to him, and his mouth turned up to smile ever so slightly. She swaddled him a bit tighter, and his mouth twitched upward a wee bit more, but Laura didn't seem to notice. "I'm sorry, if I must do something to you later," she said to Joe, and then made a hushing sound, as if Joe had indicated some kind of discomfort. She saw that an extra bottle of formula was sitting on the counter, intended for the now sleeping baby held in the arms of one of her co-workers. "Do you mind?" Laura asked, as she sat down with Joe and began to feed him.

* * *

Laura made sure the blunt and direct Nurse Director of Maternity Services, Mary Mullray, was going to be in the same room with her for the procedure. Having her there would cover both their asses, and after all, it was Mary Mullray's directive. Laura also justified punishing Mary Mullray by asking her to be in attendance, as Mary Mullray obviously wouldn't have asked Laura to perform if she'd wanted to be held responsible herself.

Joe was dressed in his onesie and diaper, was on a thin blanket, which lay flat on a cold stainless steel examining table.

"Okay, Joe," Laura said sweetly, "please don't hate me, after we're finished." She was sure that he was nodding his head quickly to indicate, *yes, I won't hate you...do what you need to do.* Laura wished she could just tell Joe a sad tale about a dead pet, or something else heartfelt, instead of doing what she had to do, so that honest waterworks would be initiated. She remembered a time, early in her job, sitting through an overhead-projector training session on the seven reasons a baby cries. Was it just last year? At the time, she thought, well, if someone needed training for something like this, they might as well work in cardiology or pediatrics—or hell, any other department where you weren't responsible for newborn babies.

Now, Laura saw the training's projections in her memory like photographs. *Hmm, if I'm being shown these for a reason, perhaps by God,* she thought, grabbing the cross on her necklace, *then, thy will be done.* She raced through her mental checklist, and what she had control over, in order to get Joe to produce a cry on his own—looking for something other than what she had been asked to do. Hunger? *I just gave him a bottle.* Wanting to be held? *Certainly, not the case.* Tired? *Not that either.* Too hot or too cold? *Hospitals are always cold. I could wrap him in many blankets to make him too hot, but he loves being wrapped up. Not viable.* Need a diaper change? *Joe has needed many diaper changes since he's been here and there is documentation of his not having cried yet...Next!* Sometimes they just feel like crying? *Ugh. Next!* In pain or doesn't feel well? *And if he can't cry ever...oh, shit.*

Laura went through the checklist again, knowing she was going to be responsible for this. She thought it through, and again, and then did so for a third time. Then, she looked at Nurse Director of Maternity Services, Mary Mullray, cursed her under her breath, and with a sterile needle in her hand, made baby Joe Gamut cry.

# Chapter Six

The Gamuts were both napping, over the sound of all the babies in the ward crying. Millie was dreaming of stacking books into a large tower, trying to prevent them from falling, and Adrian dreamt of being trapped in a large cloudy bottle of Sprite, the fizz creating loud static in his head.

"He's here! He's here!" Laura said as she entered with an inconsolable Joe, "and look what he can do!"

In actuality, Joe was a little hurt by the event, but only his feelings, because Laura never actually pricked him. It was first because of Laura's pleading and encouraging, that he began to feel betrayed. Joe wasn't quite sure why, because why would any baby want to make all that unhappy noise, which he had been hearing and noticing from all the defective babies on the ward? Why would he want to cause the same sheer panic in his parents, which all the other parents on the ward were experiencing? It seemed overwhelming to him, that shift from calm to chaos and then parental intervention—the other babies suddenly being rocked, changed, and fed, basically just to shut them up. He may have been new to the world, but Joe knew how to keep his mouth closed, and he had used all of his super baby strength to do so for the last seven days.

Yet, Joe felt weird. Here was the woman in white, whom he trusted more than any other person in his life, coaxing him to make this horrible sound of displeasure. So, he tried his hardest. Pushing out with all the power he could muster, only a squeak came out, which might have actually formed a giggle, if he were able to giggle. Then after more encouragement, Joe wondered, *Is this crying what she really wants? Is she really asking me for this?* It was only when she grabbed the sharp needle from the counter, under the bulletin board, where a poster titled *What You Should Know About Shaken Baby Syndrome* rested, that he had an epiphany. To please her, and to please everyone, he must cry, even if it was the thing which wouldn't usually please anyone. *Why would his dear woman in white want this?* For the first time in his life, Joe felt deceived, so, using all of his tiny strength, he brought on the waterworks full force.

\* \* \*

Millie was still dreaming about towers of books perfectly stacked, when the books in her dream suddenly toppled over. "What?" Millie asked, with a tone of sleepy shock, which Laura recognized as that of a new tired mother.

"He's here, and he's crying," Laura repeated. "But, I don't think he's hungry, tired, or wet."

"What do we do?" Adrian asked, his head still buzzing with white noise from his own dream.

"Oh, I know what to do," Millie said. "Give him to me. He probably just wants his Mama."

Millie received Joe in her bed and held him. He still cried. She stood up and held him. He continued. She stood up, held him and bounced him gently. That didn't work. She stood up, held him and rocked him, and he keep wailing. She tried to give him a bottle, and changed his diaper, and sang him a song of sixpence. Nothing. Finally, she offered him to Adrian, who waved her off. "I don't know what to do!" he exclaimed, pushing his glasses up to his nose, three times quickly. Millie knew what to do, but nothing seemed to be working. Joe pushed and snuggled against the thin, bleach-smelling, hospital blanket. It felt cozy to him, and Joe, still crying, felt strangely happy. He was pleased that he was doing what everyone wanted of him, and this is what life, as he would know it, was all about.

# Chapter Seven

By the time Joe was approved for discharge, the other babies on the ward were all crying more than usual. That's what happened when they were kept awake by the 24-hour howling from one Joe Gamut. His parents were exhausted, and they too, felt like crying. Laura was exhausted, but she could take breaks and walk around The Good Sam, or go home to silence after her long shift. Millie was dog-tired, but she knew that just as Joe had spent a long time not crying, he would probably spend a long time crying as well, and that it would eventually stop.

The Nurse Director of Maternity Services, Mary Mullray, knew that it had been strange to keep Joe in the hospital for not crying, but it was equally strange to discharge him for constantly crying. Still, rules were rules, and she made the rules, and rules were often made to avoid liability.

As Gamuts walked past the nursing station, they felt the staff were relieved that Joe was leaving. He had gone from the easiest baby to the most difficult in a split second. Laura jumped from her post and wrapped Millie and Joe simultaneously in one big hug. She bent down and gave Joe a kiss, and for a split second his crying stopped; he smiled, then looked at Laura, and began to cry again. In that same split second, Adrian breathed a loud sigh, which seemed like the most tired sigh ever recorded. When they reached the corner of the hall closest to the elevator, Laura peeled back the blankets which lay over two wheelchairs, covering boxes of diapers and dried formula. "Here, Adrian, why don't you push one of these," she winked. Adrian smiled, not sure if the wink was to encourage him to push, or meant something else.

Back down at ground level, Adrian intentionally walked ahead of both Millie and Laura, who were forced to nearly yell their conversation over Joe's vocalizations. Laura's long blonde hair brushed the top of a Pampers box, and she was careful not to get it tangled in the moving wheels of the chair. Near the front door, a dark-haired young man, wedged into a tight uniform, commanded Adrian to stop. Adrian froze, trying to get his glasses to rest in place, as his hands were busy with one of the wheelchairs.

"Excuse me?" the security guard snapped at Adrian, "Where are you going with these?" He reached out, and stopped the chair's advance with his hand. Adrian could still hear Joe crying, so he knew they weren't far behind him. "You thought you could stock your home with all these supplies, care of Banner Good Samaritan Hospital?" Adrian wanted to say, yes, because it was logical and it seemed like that was exactly what he was doing. Joe's cries could be heard, moving closer to them. "Why don't you push that chair over there, by the Information Desk, while I get some back-up," said the guard.

The sound of Joe's wailing resembled a police car's siren, approaching quickly from behind. When Laura saw Adrian, and the security officer barking into his walkie-talkie, she aggressively strode over and slapped the device out of his hand. "Antonio, what the hell are you doing?"

"Hey, what the hell, Laura!" he said. "I didn't...."

"What the hell?" she mimicked in an exasperated tone. "What you see in this wheelchair are charitable donations, from the good folks of Phoenix, for a very special case in our hospital. Antonio, this is Joe, and these are the Gamuts, Adrian and Millie." Antonio stood there at the point where shame overtakes anger. "Say hello to the Gamuts," Laura chided.

"Hello," Antonio said softly as his walkie-talkie squawked from the floor. Antonio picked it up. "Never mind," he told it. "10-4."

Around Antonio, Laura looked more vulnerable than Millie had seen during their seven- day stay at The Good Sam; but, then, in a flash, her confidence returned. "You know, I almost thought it was a good idea to accept your dinner invitation, until just now, when you got all macho-man on me. I was considering it, and, I know, I know, you're going to say it's all part of the job."

"Shit, Laura."

"I'm seeing someone anyway," Laura announced. Millie could tell that she wasn't, but it was a good poker play, especially against Antonio, who appeared not to be holding many cards. Adrian stayed frozen, hoping that a wink didn't mean that she was seeing *him*.

"Hunh?"

"Antonio, this is Joe Gamut, my new boyfriend." Laura laughed when she said it. Millie beamed with delight at this turn of events, and Adrian stood in place like a statue, with crooked glasses on his face, too confused by this interaction to move.

# Chapter Eight

Adrian pulled the seatbelt through, and Joe was shifted in behind the barely padded restraint bar of his new car seat. *It was like belting someone into a carnival ride*, Adrian thought. Joe still hadn't stopped crying, so the illusion was that Joe was entering a ride which was to be a terrifying experience. Adrian knew Joe would eventually stop crying, as it was impossible for him not to. Perhaps Joe was just mixed up. Adrian wished to know what was going through the mind of his newborn. What he didn't know was that his newborn had previously thought staying quiet was pleasing to others, but then the trusted woman in white had taught him that this was not the case. Joe had decided he would stay with this thought for a while.

For Adrian, it was the most stressful of rides, the constant noise a driving distraction, as well as an anxiety-provoking trigger for causing a potential accident. It was only a fifteen-minute drive home to Sunnyslope, Arizona, but to Adrian it seemed like hours. He had adjusted his glasses over a hundred times. Millie sat in the back with Joe, singing and cooing in an attempt to settle Joe. Instead, it sounded to Adrian like two different radio stations, playing jazz and punk music at the same time.

\* \* \*

During the course of the next day, Adrian and Millie, now stuck at home, had become short with one another—snapping about what to do to help their young, non-stop, displeased, now constantly-crying son. They were exhausted already, and they had not been home for long. Joe was only quiet when sleeping, which was only for a few

hours at a time, for when he awoke, after a moment of gauging his sur-
roundings, the crying started all over again. Millie had heard about
children with colic because she had seemingly read every mothering
book which ever existed. She read up on all the techniques for how
to sooth a crying baby, and none of them worked. It was so stressful at home that she now felt she had to get away from Adrian as
well. He was acting more like their distraught baby by the minute. It
wasn't until she brought a nearly exhausted Joe to the den area, and
a cartoon was on television, that Joe suddenly stopped crying.

# Chapter Nine

Joe Gamut, with what he could control, was constantly doing his best trying to please everyone. By two weeks of age, he was a 'yes' baby, especially if he could frame the situations going on around him in positive, 'yes-induced' ways. Even at birth, he wasn't saying, 'no,' to crying, he was saying, 'yes,' to not crying. Now it seemed the dark haired, slow-moving, easy-going woman, and the jagged thin man with glasses, wanted him to stop crying. *What about the woman in white? Where was she? She had some sort of part in all this, hadn't she? Hadn't she brought him into the world? She was the first to make him cry. What did he need to do now?* He was so small, and the world was so big, he just couldn't have enough control over what he needed and craved.

If he paid attention, he would get some lessons from the cartoons the soft woman and he were watching. In the glowing box, there was a group of very special people he related to. There was one who was super strong, one with a never-ending rope he threw, one who could spin around so fast he knocked people over (an action which reminded him of how the man with glasses moved). There was also one who was a silly bird, and then there was the greatest one of all, a red-haired baby in a diaper, who seemed to be their leader. That baby could stretch a nipple from a baby bottle, to propel it, and knock over all the bad guys. The baby would also drink from the bottle to become stronger. Even the strong man took time to have a few sips from the bottle to increase his own strength, just as sometimes the tolerant woman sharing the sofa with him now would sneak a taste of his formula.

Joe was fascinated. He wished to be the baby in the cartoon, to have a super power and have total control over situations. It dis-

tracted him so much that he forgot the days-old promise to please the
woman in white at the hospital, the promise he made to cry. Without
realizing it, he had stopped. But then his mother suddenly let out a
shriek, which wasn't a cry of sadness or a soothing vocal tone, but
rather something alarming which brought in the wiry guy, who immediately knocked over a lamp in the den. Joe was startled, and he
immediately started to cry again. The woman and the man had been
excited all day, first with Joe's new silence in the room, then with the
loud smashing sound, and finally with the noise of Joe crying once
more. They desperately used their soft voices to turn Joe's crying
back around. They thought that would work, but it was Joe, who
had caught another glimpse of the show *The Mighty Heroes*, which
caused his self-soothing. The heroes had spent the better part of the
show getting in each other's way and knocking each other out, similar to the chaos which just happened in the den. Now these cartoon
characters had completely come together to help each other out before the show ended. *This is what life is all about*, Joe thought. *If he
was Diaper Man, and his father, Tornado Man, his mother had to be another one of the characters, maybe Strong Man. And, if this all were true
then, maybe, they could all do something to help each other out.* Joe, for
the first time ever, had just a small moment of crying and then was
able to stop. The soft woman called him by his name, and hugged
him strongly. "You and I like the same cartoon. I think you're going
to be okay," she said to him. "I think things are turning in a good,
healthy, way."

# Chapter Ten

After much prodding from Millie, Adrian agreed that, yes, "things may turn out in a good way." That's the way they communicated, or problem-solved, and it followed extremely predictable scripts. The first was the easiest. Millie prodded until Adrian agreed, or Millie continued to prod if she felt Adrian was just agreeing to please her, or, lastly, Millie just prodded as Adrian continued to not answer or say anything, but visibly decreased his anxiety. The last outcome was Millie's favorite because it allowed her to process situations out, basically by herself, with Adrian feeling like he was participating. In this case—of her talking and his being silent—there was a certain expediting factor about that which helped them reach a conclusion. There was a big advantage to her in saying things out loud, versus keeping them inside and processing them internally.

Millie had been worried about Adrian, about his ability to deal with a challenging baby like Joe. She knew her husband was very factual and very calculating, a characteristic often popularly described as a scientific, or left-side of the brain dominant. She knew she was right-side of the brain dominant, but also felt that the best couples were a mix of people who had opposite sides of brains dominant. *Put two right-sides together and all hell could break loose*, she always thought. Millie worried Joe's traits would "not compute" to Adrian, or possibly they would all compute and be too much for him to handle. *His brain would burst into flames*, she thought. Even his job as Chief Accountant at Legend City Theme Park, the western based park, which incorporated all of his skills, was something beyond Adrian's comfort zone. It was the first job he had applied for, when the world was just him, and Millie, a baby only a thought, or possibility, in their future.

When Adrian first started, he discovered that Legend City Theme Park was the area's largest (and only) amusement park, but somehow, the park never managed to do well financially. Immediately, Adrian had some understanding of what needed to be done to fix that, but he never made any suggestions, as that was not his role. His job was only to crunch the numbers in the accounting books. The boss, Charles Capel, was the one who should have been doing more along the lines of fixing things. Charles was in charge, but under his leadership, the payroll was often missed, and creditors were banging on their door. On most Fridays, the employees would leave the parking area as if it were a gumball rally, racing to the bank to cash their checks before the payroll account hit zero. Capel himself wasn't the model of confidence to his employees, driving around in a beat up, often broken down, Mitsubishi L-300 van, which was rumored to be one of his perks from Capel's buying out Mitsubishi. Mitsubishi, the previous owners of Legend City, had abandoned the western theme of the park, as they only wanted Legend City to feature Mitsubishi's technology and computer synchronization of the amusement rides. Many of the rides they installed featured cartoon cats. Logically, a theme park in Phoenix should have had a decent probability of success, but given the poor numbers, Adrian arrived home and fretted about both what was happening, and more importantly, the logical reasons why. First and foremost, the park was only open during the day, and Phoenix was often as hot as one hundred degrees in the sun. More than a few times, the guests of Legend City passed out from heat, dehydration, and in one case, near-death from sun-stroke.

It was during these times that Millie was able to intercede with logic, reassuring Adrian that he had the type of skills and education that any company would want, especially in an up and coming city such as Phoenix. After all, didn't he land the job at Legend City, with its easy twelve minute commute, almost immediately upon their moving to Sunnyslope? Rationally, it made a lot of sense, that there were other close-by jobs in case Legend City didn't work out, and that he should enjoy his employment there until it ran out. This kept Adrian relaxed until there was a pay period where there were no checks to be cashed, and they all had to wait another week. The irregularity of that week upset Adrian, because he and Millie were planning to have a baby, so, at that point, the finances needed to be consistent and predictable.

Millie told him not to worry, said that he would end up in much better shape in the long run without Charles Chapel. If Legend City went belly-up, he would be hired at a new job, with real options to go up the ladder and earn much more money. Chapel would be the one who'd be ruined. Millie convinced him that if he wanted to look around at other employment now, a change would be more lucrative than what he was doing currently. Millie's support, along with his predictable daily lunch at one of the two on-site restaurants, El Sombrero or The Dog House, helped Adrian get through the day. It was at night that he became nervous, but it was nothing that Millie couldn't fix, not that fixing people was her job. To her it was all about feeling empathy, and she had undying empathy toward all—a wish to make them all feel comfortable and accepted unconditionally. It was all these wonderful things that made Millie perfect in Adrian's eyes.

Millie also wanted to be a good parent. She always thought her parents were perfect textbook examples of this. They were two people who always communicated. But she knew now that there were things less than perfect that were still *good*, and good was perfectly fine. Even though the three modes of communication she experienced with Adrian were not ideal, all of them served a purpose and got things done. This was something that both a left-dominant, and a right-dominant brain could grasp completely, in their own separate ways.

# Chapter Eleven

Even within a perfect world of understanding, and a perfect world of individuals, love is a difficult concept to grasp. Some may think love is a head-over-heels attraction from the beginning to the end of a relationship which, when that part fades, as it often does, indicates time to end the relationship. This was especially true for others during the time period of Adrian and Millie's marriage, when the divorce rate was in the middle of a high spiking. The marriages in Millie's parents' generation were financially and morally built to last. Her father, Richard, being the breadwinner, reinforced a common dynamic which forced the women to stay in order to survive. Samantha, her mother, was the caretaker, commonly known at the time as the housewife.

Even as a young girl, Millie had a difficult time with the term *housewife*. It somehow inferred that her mother, who was a model of independence, was bound to a house, based on her role as a woman being dependent upon a man. She imagined a different world where her mother would introduce her father at events as her *equally-working-husband*. It seemed better that way. Samantha's role as housewife was one she had had to grow into, but never fully accepted. She and her husband had not planned for Millie, and Samantha, at the time, managed a retail store, making almost as much money as Richard. Before Millie, they traveled, spoke openly to one another with respect regarding their equality as partners. When Millie popped into the world, Samantha acknowledged her new role, not because she loved it, but rather because she loved Millie above anything else, and no nanny could ever be as loving toward Millie as she was. This is what unselfish love meant to her.

The love Millie's parents had between them was of the head-over-heels variety. Everyone noticed how they interacted, how they hung on each other's every word, and how locked their eyes were upon one another. It was the obvious love, which became idealized from the nineteen-sixties, and which ultimately, history found, was measured by disappointment, and later divorce. But this, in Richard and Samantha Englander's case, never happened. Richard and Samantha also incorporated the conviction that their love could not be replaced by any other person, place, or thing.

In her own marriage, Millie saw the basic nuts and bolts in her relationship with Adrian as being similar to what they were in the relationship between her mother and father. She saw the reasoning and respect part of their love as the glue which held it together. She saw the open-mindedness in how they dealt with day-to-day decisions, and she loved that part of it. She loved Adrian a lot. She loved his logic. She loved that she logically fit into his life plan. She loved that he considered her to be warm. She loved being the opposite of the coldness he hated, one which brought back memories of his own isolation. She loved every basic thing about his basicness. She wasn't sure about his attractiveness. That would fall into the category of 'sometimes.' Adrian, after all, had average height, average weight, with just a touch of flab. Genetically he had thin hair which was dirty blonde, almost oddly gray. He wore a suit and button down shirts during the day, and a tee-shirt and slacks at night. He wore inexpensive glasses. How unspectacular was that?

In the bedroom, she was in charge, which she liked. She liked taking them to a place of reckless abandon. They would make love when she wanted, and only when she initiated. She loved pretty much all of his basicness, because basic was easily something she could dominate. The best part was that his basicness made her feel safe, and all she had to do, really, was settle down his worries, soothe his overall anxiety. For Millie, a person with boundless compassion, it came pretty easy. Even when they argued, Millie still was able to see both sides of it.

Adrian thought she was the woman he had hand-picked, even though he didn't. (To him, the thought of them being together just seemed like a logical outcome, so Millie let it slide because they were *simpatico*.) When he was cold, she was warm. When he was worried, she was reassuring. When he was fast, she was slow. When he needed to list reasons, she would listen. When he was detached,

she would make love to him. She had most of the control, though
he thought he had it. Even when he asked Millie to marry him, it
was only after he had calculated a 100% reasonable conclusion that
she would say 'yes.' In her psychological, well rounded view of the
world, a view much more liberal than Adrian's absolutes, his 100%
might be only 75%. But to her, 75% was a pretty solid percentage.
Rationally, Adrian was always aware of those differentials, making
their marriage something he had to work hard on. She liked that he
had to increase his bottom line minimally at the very least, by 25%,
to conclusively reach the equivalent numeric value of their marriage,
the value which he had fostered in his head.

# Chapter Twelve

Laura felt a strange emptiness at work after Joe left. *He's just a baby, she thought, but why does this baby feel special?* At her job there were babies, and then there were more babies, and then there were new babies...babies...babies, all day and all night. She even dreamt of babies—feeding them, or feeding them things they shouldn't eat, such as steak. She dreamt of dropping them—or trying to help them, but being locked out of the nursery when the babies needed her. The nightmare she had last week was being pistol-whipped by a baby. At home, she thought she would open up a cabinet and find babies in them. Fuck, there were babies everywhere.

She found that when she took time off from work, and had perspective, she loved babies more than anything. It was the job which caused her resentments, always having to use that calm voice, always the repetition of what it takes to care for basically an amoeba—that pooped, and cried. There was too much of a difference between being at The Good Sam, and being herself.

The week when Joe was in the hospital, she learned that not all babies cried. Sometimes they only cried when you ordered them to...*wait*, she thought. *I never pricked Joe. Why did he suddenly begin crying, and then why didn't he stop?* She wondered if he was still crying at his new home, or if he was there as silent as a bug. She was still amazed and fascinated by him, even though she no longer was his nurse at The Good Sam.

After the pistol-whip dream, Laura wondered if she might be in the wrong field of nursing. She wondered what field combined taking care of people, being kind, and being herself. *Perhaps some sort of psychiatric nursing*, she thought. Ironically, it was Joe, the baby, who may have kindled that interest in her.

She also pondered because of her dream whether she was watching the wrong movies at the Multi-Plex. Laura enjoyed the simplicity of going to them alone. The last movie she took herself to was a little gem called *Vigilante*. It's the story of a New York City factory worker, who was a solid citizen and regular guy until the day a sadistic street gang brutally assaulted his wife and murdered their child. The thugs were not convicted, and were sent back onto the streets, where, of course, they were all killed, one-by-one, by the factory worker. She loved the psychology of it. How a person, in this case a solid citizen, had to adjust to a world he never could have imagined. Laura also enjoyed the pure violence in these movies, and that made her feel guilty. She needed to confess that the next time she met with the priest from her parish, who, puzzled, did not give her even one Hail Mary, or an Our Father, to atone for these sins. *Vigilante* also made her glad she lived in Arizona, because New York seemed like an isolating and ghastly place.

When she left the theater that night, she was approached by a man, about her age, who had specifically asked her about sitting by herself. She knew the answer, locked and loaded, which would shut him down.

"Look, it's not that I can't get a date or don't have friends, because I have many of both. I do things by myself, without any hassle. I love movies, just not movie dates, because–why go somewhere with someone you might be interested in and not talk to them for two to three hours?" It seemed way too wordy, and the man just stood there, which made her feel stupid. "And I just wanted to be out of the house, as I was getting stir crazy sitting there by myself," she quickly added into the dead air. She realized that she might have made a mistake, making herself prey for this stranger. She wished she had a gun, like the vigilante, that could be her judge and her jury if he turned out to be dangerous. She then thought, *why am I so nervous? I get approached all the time.*

The stranger, who had been at the same movie with some friends, sensed the situation and tried a different approach, "I'm sorry, I didn't mean to worry you. That was a pretty scary movie, wasn't it?"

"Yes," Laura stated, without fear.

"Look. My name is Steven. Can I ask for your number? If you want, you can give me a fake number right now, but I really hope you will give me your real number and make it possible to call you."

"Well, Steven, I wouldn't do that. I must admit, I hadn't thought of that," she said. "If I wanted to, I would have just given you my number and then worked around your calls in some way. I'm good at letting the answering machine take it and decide whether to call back."

"Okay, you can do that," he laughed, "or you can do what I suggested, but either way, I'm going to walk away after I get your real, or a fake, number."

"Here," she said, giving Steven her real telephone number.

# Chapter Thirteen

Joe felt love when his parents wrapped him snugly in his blanket, with his arms and legs bound, with only his little head peeking out of the top. He felt love again, when Millie wrapped a fresh diaper on him, and taped it as tight as it would go. He had to act displeased in order to get them to do either of these, but most of the time he passively lay there and pleased them. He was quiet most of the time, the easy baby everyone thought he was earlier in the hospital, but having to use that damn displeasure in order to communicate need? What God invented *that*?

He was getting bigger. The hospital blankets, which Laura had supplied the family with in numbers enough for ten babies, were not as effectively binding him as they used to. Joe tried to stay still and enjoy the cocoon, but an appendage here and there would jut out creating something a little out of balance in the wonderful sheltered world he wanted. It was uncomfortable.

Then, there was a new kind of covering. This one didn't feel good at all. They were called socks. On Joe's feet, they were tight, and felt as rough as if they were made from millions of pinheads. Kicking them off provided only temporary relief. *If only socks were bigger, like covering my full body. I would love that*, he thought. So, solving the sock problem by kicking them off created a new problem. Now it was the air, which often attacked a newly exposed, foot or unbound hand, and maybe, bothered him all the way up to his shins and forearms. He tried to be a good baby, so he attempted to communicate, with his eyes, that he wanted to be tightly wrapped. He pointed his eyes, where he wanted his parents to attend to, but it felt that he couldn't stretch his eyeballs far enough to convey his wish. *What the hell*, he thought. *Diaper Man's crew could stretch their eyes*. So, he tried using his arms. This didn't work either, as he had limited control over them, and his arms just flailed around instead of being able to functionally point. In addition, flailing caused his arm to be outside the blanket, which was already not snug enough to completely inhibit him, so he had to deal once again with the air; the painful, uncomfortable air.

Then, Joe would cry. It was a normal cry, but not for the normal baby reasons. Joe would cry not for any reason on Laura's training list, but rather from his conflict: he knew that quiet would please his parents, but he needed to be heard, to satisfy his wants and needs.

He recently saw an episode of *The Mighty Heroes* in which two good guys were turned into monsters by a device, creating more bad guys to be used for bad things. The machine was run by an evil person named The Monsterizer. It reminded Joe of the hospital again, where all the babies were loud and crying, and turned into monsters, until the nurses grabbed bottles to shut them up. Diaper Man had stopped The Monsterizer from starting the device by hitting him with his milk bottle. *Why be part of the problem, when you can be part of the solution?* Joe thought. Thus, even if he had to try to do things the way everyone else did, Joe wasn't sold on the human method of communication being all that functional.

# Part II

# Chapter One

Millie Englander was a typical and basically unplanned child from Richard and Samantha Englander. She was born in the mid nineteen-fifties, in Cambridge, Massachusetts, which was a fine place to grow up in. She had brown hair, brown eyes, and bulkier than average legs. To say she was her parents' mistake would be a bit of a gaffe, as they never made her feel anything less than a treasured jewel. Still, her parents, older in years than most, never spoiled her the way others parents spoiled only children. Instead, she received life's lessons, including the nuts and bolts of being strong no matter the circumstances.

Millie was under flexible parental reins, not prohibited from attempting anything she might possibly dream. Millie could be whatever her thoughts and visions conjured up. Richard and Samantha never closed the door on any option for her, being the typical, old-fashioned, Massachusetts liberals which they were. Millie could play with trucks, or she could play with dolls, and wear pink, but only when she wanted to, which was rare and always felt uncomfortable.

Richard and Samantha were open, communicative, and social. It seemed to Millie that they were speaking to each other constantly, except when they were asleep, or watching a television show together. At those times, there was total silence. They even called each other "R," and "S," so that they wouldn't waste their breath on saying the full names. There was so much more for breaths to be used on.

Although on the left side politically, her parents didn't believe in the revolts and protests of the nineteen-sixties. They understood the desire of people for something better, and the wish to change things which weren't right. But they thought violence was never necessary, as there were always better ways for members of a society to get things done.

After school, Millie could hold her own on the sandlot with neighborhood boys, so Richard and Samantha signed her up for Little League. Because she was a girl, they knew it meant fighting for her right to participate. On sign-up night, Richard and Samantha were so engaged in their conversation with each other, that Richard interrupted her while she filled out the paperwork; thus the name on the sheet was written as Mill, spelled without the "i.e." Cambridge Little League knew no better, so when the coach called to welcome what he thought was a boy named "Miller" onto the Tigers, Millie could barely wait until they held their first practice. She prepared her hair in braids; wore the Detroit Tigers hat her father bought her, and ran across O'Donnell Field, only to be met by a disoriented coach. That day in practice, she lined a few hits, vacuumed up some infield grounders, and raced around the diamond as fast as her legs would take her. Then on Monday, the Englanders got the call telling her she had been disqualified from the Cambridge Little League.

It seemed, according to the caller, that she would do much better in the all-girls softball division. She was assigned to a team named "The Pink Petunias." Millie protested, but Richard and Samantha told her to give it a shot. "Sometimes things end up how they end up, and it's okay to make the best of it and be an example for all the others," they said.

When it was time for The Pink Petunias' first practice, Millie, in her Tigers hat, quickly grew deflated when she saw her new team wearing pink hats, without any lettering or emblems. The team also didn't seem to be any good. They had difficulty both catching and throwing the ball, and Millie could see they missed most of the pitched balls, swinging like rusty old gates. Their coach, having been briefed on Millie's abilities, was very excited to have her there. Millie seemed like the perfect person to save the Pink Petunias from their lack of aptitude. Millie was uninterested in that role, and less interested in softball, so immediately after practice, she quit.

Her mother took her aside and reinforced that her decision was a positive one, not just for her, but for women everywhere. The about face surprised her, but actually it was always about doing the right thing all along. "Look honey," her mother said, "This is not quitting. I thought that playing softball and being an example of a strong female athlete would be okay, but I think it's more about you being happy, and not accepting less than ideal situations forced upon you by men. You know, impact can often be found in just leaving and not participating in the injustice. By not playing softball, you aren't producing a big nothing. Doing nothing is, in fact, doing something. Forcing or having conflict about things that aren't what they should be can be exhausting."

Millie gave her mother a hug. "I will be an example, especially to the ones who can't speak up for themselves. I will be the one that will speak up for them."

# Chapter Two

From their different points of view and measures, Millie and Adrian both thought Joe was extremely smart—not just in the way most parents felt their own babies were *genius smart*, but actually finding evidence that he was. Joe was a virtuoso in seeing the purpose of things around him and incorporating them into his world. For example, Joe never crawled. Joe pushed himself around the house on his stomach or his back. His legs became very strong from all this pushing. Adrian had a concern that his lack of crawling might indicate some developmental delay, but before he could conclude that it *did*, Joe was suddenly sitting up. Then, on the same day, he was up on two feet, leaning against the sofa, cruising. A day later, he was standing on his own.

In a week, Joe began to toddle around, which for parents is a stressful time. Adrian was already stressed by focusing on developmental issues, but now was certainly more stressed about the house not yet being baby-proofed—a need which happened way too suddenly.

He was never 100% sure about developmental issues. He remembered being a small boy, and his parents describing him as being in a fog. He was even brought to a doctor who concluded that there was nothing really wrong with him. His parents then determined that perhaps it was his vision, that maybe he wasn't seeing things clearly. Of course, the doctor could not measure that. Little Adrian was so uncomfortable in his own skin that he wanted to scream, which forced him to stay in his own head a lot. When he stayed there, he would feel safe—but he could not handle things outside of that box well at all. Even during elementary school recess, Adrian would find himself alone, outside the groups playing kickball, tag, or flipping baseball cards. Adrian knew that to be included he'd have to interact. No one was going to ask him, but somehow he *needed* the prompting. He could not do it on his own. The other kids didn't know to do this because most kids don't need to be invited to play at recess. So Adrian hung around just on the outskirts of various groups of kids involved in their games—hoping to be asked to join. But then, after he'd stood there for 30 minutes, the bell would ring, and recess was over. One day, he took some of his baseball cards out of his pocket, so that everyone would know he was available to flip with them—without having to ask anyone. He still wasn't asked by anyone.

* * *

Once Millie jumped into action, baby-proofing for Adrian was a breeze. Joe did not seem to be overtly curious about the normal, potentially dangerous, household landmines. Joe was uninterested in opening cabinets which held such things as dishwasher detergent and other poisons. He would not stick his fingers into, or even near, electrical outlets. No baby gates were needed as the house had no stairs or basement areas.

The Gamuts' home, at 29 West Sunnyslope Lane, was built in the early 1960s. It was a small, white, and sunny ranch, with a covering Millie thought looked like a carport, shielding the front door from the sun. Their front yard was clay-colored stones, and the back was desert dirt, which kicked up whenever the wind became slightly more than a breeze. Adrian was familiar with what grew in the hot Arizona weather, but Millie had suggested they plant grass when they first moved in. Although Adrian had teased her, it wasn't until the cost of landscaping was quoted to her that she gave up on the idea. It was times like those she missed Boston; but she hadn't wanted to be married to a complaining, cantankerous, Popsicle, which is what Adrian would have been if they stayed close to Boston University. Also, there weren't too many affordable areas for them to live in there, when they were just starting out.

Right after graduation Adrian favored any job at a location which featured a warm climate, but as luck would have it, Legend City had an opening for an accountant. Being back in the area near where he grew up was also comforting to him, and not just because of the weather. Sunnyslope was an area of Phoenix which seemed to have a rich history—not at all comparable to Boston, but still, it was something.

In the early 1900s, before there was a Sunnyslope, its founder, William Norton, had been enjoying a buggy ride over the desert, with his daughter, close to the North Mountains. It was a typical beautiful day in that area of Arizona. Mr. Norton's daughter looked at the sun shining on the mountains, and exclaimed, "My! What a pretty sunny slope." Norton liked the phrase so much that he named the town Sunny Slope (two words at the time), and in 1911 he plotted out the first sector of development, which grew slowly, to only four to five cottages, in the first eight years.

Adrian always liked the story, and the separate identity of the now one-worded Sunnyslope. It stayed that way even when the City of Phoenix annexed it, and it remained standing as a community on its own.

* * *

As it turned out, besides not touching dangerous items, Joe was not big on toys either. The only things he was curious about were the smooth white and clay-colored stones and pebbles, laid out in the front and back yards of the house. He liked to sit on the ground, measuring the heat within those stones. Some were hot to his skin, some were warm, and some, in the morning, under the door's canopy, were cool against his bare legs. Sometimes he would pick up a few stones and press them against his tee-shirt. Millie and Adrian usually kept the door open for Joe to leave any time he wanted, as he never wished to stray too far from the house. Joe seemed only to want to flop down on the stones which lay on the ground.

Millie was curious about ground cover too. In other locations in the United States where grass could not be grown, there were other kinds of replacements. She remembered seeing bleached seashells in Florida, the one time her family had taken a week in the warm weather, a little break from the New England climate and cement of Cambridge. Although they had enjoyed it, her parents were not the type to leave home and retire there permanently. *Hell*, Millie thought. *They would be happy having more time in an empty room together, anywhere; it wouldn't matter, as long as they could chat constantly.*

Now, the concept of grass seemed strange to her. Even when Adrian took her to The Cactus League games in Diablo Stadium, it looked to her like it was rolled-on, an artificial carpet inside some obscenely gaudy and sterile office setting.

"Now, Millie, you're not making any sense," Adrian told her. Adrian only liked baseball because he could manipulate the statistical numbers in his head. He thought Millie would appreciate going, because she had wanted grass at 29 Sunnyslope Lane for a long time. "The grass is real, and why would an office install fake grass?"

"No, Adrian," she said. "I don't mean Astro-Turf; in terms of carpet, I mean *real* carpet, but I don't mean real carpet. What I mean is, visually it is like... oh, I give up."

Millie, when there weren't things to process through the methods she used with Adrian, would often become frustrated at his flat-lined inability to be creative. Adrian, though, was more than happy to bring her into his world of preciseness.

"Look, Millie," he said calmly. "When this game ends, we can walk on the grass, and you can see for yourself." When it came to matters of logic, Adrian could be as laid back as a faint breeze. When the game ended and the walk began, Millie sat down in short left-field, the blades as soft as a painter's brush massaging her thick legs. "Now that's grass," she said. "Again, you managed to make 100% sense."

\* \* \*

At home, when Millie sat just inside the screen door, and watched Joe on the rocks, she understood that he too, was processing. He certainly was unable to ask her questions, as he had yet to say his first word, but he was taking in the sensation, the data, as her husband called it, of the stones against his bare legs or chest. That conclusion made sense for her, but to Joe, well, he just liked the different types of warmth, and wished he could wrap himself up tightly in a suit made of warm stones. Joe had begun to equate warmth, and confinement, with safety.

He also was looking for Kryptonite, and simultaneously relating the safety of warmth and confinement to superheroes, who needed to know their weaknesses—especially Superman. In the past few months, he had advanced his obsession from Diaper Man to Superman. Superman was just a fantastic guy, Joe knew, but the variety of Superman shows and cartoons was a concept he was just beginning to experience. Superman also was a regular guy in disguise, which was amazing. It was just so much more real than Diaper Man. Joe was still in diapers, which made Diaper Man still relatable, but Superman seemed to cross new and uncharted territories.

Even the Superman cartoons had variety. Besides the early forty-year-old Superman cartoons he enjoyed, there was the *Super Friends* cartoon, which displayed a more serious version of friendship and loyalty than *The Mighty Heroes* had. The *Super Friends* were companions who actually got things done instead of messing things up. Messing things up tended not to please anyone, even when the outcome of *The Mighty Heroes* episodes were always good.

He also loved *Superman: The Movie*. It amazed his mother that he was able to sit through the long movie, entirely, without making a peep.

There was also the strange dull, colorless, television show, *The Adventures of Superman*. This version of Superman was his favorite, and the lack of color in the show, along with this version of Clark Kent, reminded Joe of his father. He thought that there was a chance his basic, "black-and-white" dad left every morning to do amazing good deeds for the world. Didn't he wear the glasses? It was an exciting thought for Joe, his dad morphing into Superman. He knew he had to make sure that there was no Kryptonite near their house, waiting to weaken or harm his father. Every day after his dad left, Joe sat outside and sifted through the white and clay-colored stones, to make sure there were none which would cause any detriment.

# Chapter Three

Adrian had no idea why Joe liked to sit in the stones and pebbles outside their house, and he was becoming concerned. He understood the reason Millie sat in the outfield of Diablo Stadium, because she missed grass, but what could Joe feel like he was missing when he sat in gravel? He was a boy and had no experiences with gravel. There was no logical conclusion to be made, and when Adrian listed, in his head, all of the reasons sitting on stones didn't make sense, the act further baffled him.

a) Small stones are not comfortable to sit on.

b) There were so many better things to be playing with, such as toys.

c) There is not much engagement, either physical or mental, when sitting outside on stones and pebbles.

d) Poisonous snakes can be found living in stone or rock beds.

Millie thought that what Joe did was not abnormal at all, and said all children were different. "He's just processing," she would remind him, "and you should understand that sometimes children run through various theories in their little heads before they can conclude something. Children learn about their world through play."

"Such as learning that rocks really aren't very exciting?" Adrian raised his arm satirically, in an exaggerated way, in pompous proclamation, which caused his glasses to fall off his face and onto the turquoise carpet.

"Maybe they are exciting to a geologist," she countered, turning away from him and striding into the kitchen.

"Maybe there's something more going on? Something could be not quite right here? Perhaps?"

"Adrian, I can't hear you," she added, intentionally running water in the sink.

"I said, maybe something isn't quite right. We went from total silence to him crying all the time, and now he is showing a preference for sitting outside on a bunch of stones."

Millie knew that Adrian was becoming tense. Usually she opted to soothe him before he continued in this direction, but this time she opted not to. "There is nothing *not quite right* with our son," she said. "Just look at how he watches his shows. He can watch *Superman* for hours, and he seems to really be in tune with it. What other kids have an attention span like that?"

"I'm not saying he's not smart. He is very smart. What I am—"

"He is smart. Very, very smart," Millie interrupted.

"Shouldn't he be saying something like 'mama' or 'dada' by now? According to the facts, this happens around six months, and walking is supposed to happen after that."

"As long as he's smart, the rest of it will come on its own. Not everything happens the same way, at the same time with everyone. I mean, look at you."

"What about me?"

"When I look at Joe, I see him wired in a lot of ways that you are wired—so I don't think there's anything wrong with where Joe is at right now. I don't think there's anything wrong with how you are," she replied, but then, she thought, *actually, I do think there are some things a little wrong. I'm just being a good spouse for overlooking them.*

"Well, fine," Adrian said, thinking that his wife's point made perfect sense, but still feeling unsettled. "I just want us to work on initiating speech with him, rather than watching shows or sitting outside on the damn rocks."

"Well, fine. I just hope when you say *us* working on it, that you actually mean *us*, and not just me."

"You're the psych major," he said, "but, write out a script of what you'll do and say to Joe to bring desired results, and I'll follow the script. You know I will. We should be consistent."

"Of course, you will," she said validating both the fact and her disappointment in how it was going to be set forth into action.

# Chapter Four

Often, when Adrian looked at Millie, he wondered how he could have been lucky enough to have ended up with someone like her. She seemed so free in his eyes, and Adrian knew he was the kind of person who stayed within the rules of society and lived straight by the book. If things were even slightly off, it would cause him a noticeable twinge of anxiety. He didn't mind that he was viewed as an egghead, or a nerd. That part never bothered him because it was so obvious. Millie, on the other hand was equal to, or perhaps even higher in intelligence than he, but it was less noticeable, and she was certainly humble about it. Those traits, along with her kind, open spirit, made Adrian feel warmth deep inside, and had originally attracted him to her.

They were both students at Boston University when they met. Adrian, a mature, independent boy from Arizona, studying account-ing, noticed Millie in, of all places, a psychology class. It was a course required for her major, but an elective for his, a class he thought might be fun. In class, he was quiet, and she, participatory—characteristics they had noticed about one another during the semes-ter.

By chance one day, they found each other sitting at the same ta-ble studying at Mugar Memorial Library, and they nodded to one another in recognition. Soon they were stealing glances from each other, between their paragraphs and balance sheets. The next day, Adrian brought to the library an extra coffee, a Coffee-Mate creamer, and various choices of sweetener for whatever her taste demanded. Later, when he looked over, he liked that she chewed on the wooden stirrer while writing notes, pulling back her brown hair occasionally with her left hand. It was almost as if her gnawing indicated a deeper appreciation of the cup of coffee he had surprised her with.

For Adrian, attending classes and meeting Millie was the best part of Boston. He hated the winter weather and the stand-off chilliness of the people. He was not used to standing outside in the cold—to wait for a Green-Line train to take him up Commonwealth Avenue. He felt like a frozen metal pole, wrapped in a loose-fitting sheet. No matter what he did, he never felt warm or covered up enough. On one of the coldest days in the history of Boston, Adrian and Millie studied together at Mugar Memorial until it closed. Finals were approaching and they both wanted to excel. Afterward, Adrian waited at the T stop for the train back to Brighton, tears from the cold rolling down his face. Adrian had not known that this involuntary response, seeming much like crying, was possible. He had to keep pulling the large, oval, wire-rim glasses off to wipe the moisture off of his face. Damn, he wished he never had to feel this cold again.

Adrian felt like he was in hell, but that was not logical for him. Hell was engulfed in flames, and here, it was so cold. He certainly was not on fire. He considered the possibility of his blood solidifying, the way that even something as turbulent as Niagara Falls did in the dead of winter. It was dark on the train platform, and he was aggressively digging into the cement with his feet–to avoid being pulled down Commonwealth Avenue by the wind–when Millie saw him. She was crossing, heading back to her dorm in Tower C, thinking, for once, it was nice that they piped heat in there so generously. When she approached, he could almost feel her compassion toward him. She asked if he missed the warmth of Phoenix, his family, and possibly his friends. Even though they saw each other daily, they hardly knew each other, and logically, the thought of saying 'no,' crossed Adrian's mind, but when Millie said, "Why don't you come over and warm up," he said, 'yes,' instead. When he woke up beside her the next morning, for the first time since he could remember, he didn't feel like an outcast or an alien. He felt what he thought was love, which contradicted everything he had experienced since his parents died. Generally, he had read that it was not a sign of stability to have felt this as quickly as he had, but there was something discernible there. There was a trust he had in her, that he could talk and be heard, and not just be processing and analyzing the social world which he had trouble understanding. She was perfect in so many ways. He loved her perfect averageness, the way that nothing really stood out, physically or emotionally. She was a woman he felt good enough for, and this was, for Adrian, the greatest thing ever.

Adrian didn't wait long, almost immediately after they were intimate, to tell her about his childhood, how he'd been home when the police came to inform him of the accident, and the aftermath of that tragedy. He told her generally about the overall treatment he had received from the too-many-to-bond-with foster parents he'd experienced. He said his brains earned him a full scholarship at Boston University, and being accepted into their program made him feel valued again. He articulated to her his main problems, which were completely social. To him, even the most basic social interactions were occurring as if he had not been given the playbook everyone else had. When he released all of these truths to Millie, it seemed to him that he was delivering a speech he had spent the last six years writing, but never wanted to recite. It came out strong, flat, and purposeful. To Adrian's surprise, it was Millie who reacted, and in a way totally opposite of his reaction. She cried, and clutched onto him, in the tiny twin bed, kissing his face and his neck the rest of the night.

\* \* \*

Adrian became a known person at her dorm, in Tower C. It was a large building, and combined with Towers A and B, housed about 1800 students. He was such a regular, it got to the point many of residents in the complex recognized him and thought he lived there. He also brushed up on all the inside information while he was there, to use in light casual conversation. "It was rumored that Tower C was made up of all the leftover parts of Towers A and B," he liked to tell people, reciting the lore of the residents.

Though conversationally useful, and amusing, that fact rang pretty true to him, as he had always felt he grew up with the leftover pieces of society. Now, with Millie in his life, Adrian no longer felt like he himself was built of spare parts. He felt warm and safe when he was with Millie, and not because Tower C was kept above eighty-five degrees between the first of November and the first of April. Logically, Adrian felt he could build up a wonderful personal routine around her, one which he hoped would last the rest of their lives.

# Chapter Five

On Laura's date with Steven, they went to The Tee Pee, a Mexican restaurant in the Arcadia section of Phoenix. Laura couldn't help wanting to call the place "The Pee Pee" in her head, and she was dying to say the joke out loud to Steven, just to see whether he would laugh or not. She then dismissed the idea, as this was their first date, and her silly sense of humor might not go over. Connecting the restaurant with urine might be a deal-breaker, especially since Steven loved the food here. *Don't you have to have a deal, in order to break it,* Laura thought. *What a funny term, as if we made a deal before the first date even happened, and I would be the one to break it by calling The Tee Pee by a funny name.*

She kept her mouth shut. Laura didn't want to risk the date going poorly. She wanted it to go well so she had something to ward off Neanderthal Antonio, the security guard at Banner Good Samaritan Hospital, because if she were in a relationship it would give him less of a chance to bully her into a date with him.

The Tee Pee Restaurant had been around forever. Its vinyl red booths reminded Laura of the out-of-the-way places old-timers like Frank Sinatra would have secret meetings at with their mobster friends. That was, of course, if Sinatra had mob connections, and his mob connections liked Mexican food, and also, of course, if he lived in Phoenix. Laura listened to the history of The Tee Pee, as told by Steven, who loved the place so much that the owners Kathy and Zip knew him by name and stopped by to say hello. Laura thought Steven did this to impress her, but it was such a cheesy, manipulative move, that she quickly ruled it out.

At the table she suddenly laughed thinking of the word pee-pee; the laughter caused her blonde hair to flow softly over her face so she had to flip it back over her shoulder. *Damn*, she thought, *even at a Mexican restaurant, work terminology had entered her mind*. When you worked in the maternity ward, you never said urine; you said pee-pee instead.

"What are you thinking about?" Steven asked.

"Oh, nothing," she said.

"You're laughing. Did the margaritas hit you funny?"

"I'm just thinking about work, but maybe the margaritas *are* hitting me. I'm such a light weight."

"Oh, I see. So what's so funny?"

Steven was a psychologist, so Laura was a bit unnerved answering his questions. He was the one in power, and even if it might only be safe banter she wasn't quite sure how he was evaluating her. She wondered if his probing questions, which put her on the defensive, were questions of interest or qualifiers of some diagnoses he had been considering for her. Maybe hearing her answers Steven would conclude that she actually was as crazy as she sometimes thought she was. Certainly, she didn't want any validation in the area of her craziness, so she took a serious tack and talked strictly and professionally about her job. She talked about babies and what is was like helping the mothers and these babies. She told him that, in general, she was getting sick of mothers and babies, and that her job was ruining babies for her. Laura told him that she was no longer sure she wanted to have a baby of her own, at any time in the future.

It was Steven's turn to get defensive, since he saw her conversation as a first date screening test for compatibility. He sensed it was a backdoor to, *how do you feel about marriage and a long-term commitment with someone that may not want to have a baby?* So he dodged, and said, "Oh, is that so?" Then Laura continued, and began to tell him about Joe. Laura said that it was a strange, unusual, and the most amazing bond she ever felt with a newborn. She explained the uniqueness of the situation and how heartbreaking it was to be asked to do something unethical. She went on to say that Joe managed, on his own, to start to cry, as if he understood what she wanted him to do. What she felt almost immediately was that Joe was like the love she'd been searching for her entire life; and now, sitting with Steven, she realized that yes, even early on a first date, she should begin to have some sort of emotional response to him as well.

But he cut her off and noted that maybe she was in the wrong field of nursing, which made her wonder how he knew about her doubts. The margaritas were heavy on the tequila, and Laura was slightly buzzed, forgetting that before she spoke about Joe, she basically had complained about her job. In Laura's mind, it was synchronistic events such as this which made two people connect initially. It had worked that way with her and Joe, and now a tiny initial ignition had started, which might develop into a spark with Steven.

# Chapter Six

Joe was having a strange sense of *déjà vu* when his parents were taking turns asking him to "Say, 'mama,'" or "Say, 'dada.'" It reminded him of the last demand he was prompted to obey, from Laura, only without the betrayal of hurt caused by the threat of a pushpin. The parental parroting all seemed really repetitive, boring to him, and not nearly as functional as crying, which directly communicated something he was feeling. *Say, mama or dada? Did these people not know who they were? Why was it so urgent to label them?*

It seemed rather arbitrary to Joe, because he wasn't being asked to say wall, crib, bottle, television or anything else. Plus what happened if he made the wrong choice? Would someone's feelings get hurt? If he said "mama" first, would his dad feel sad? This was no time for conflict and he wished they'd stop. It was also interfering with his *Superman* show watching, and Superman was the most important person in the world. What would the world do without Superman? He was so essential, so calm, cool, and collected.

At least when his mother prompted him, she too, was calm and collected. His father seemed a little stressed out, and demanding, spewing orders rather than making a request of him. Joe knew that this was life, but he was so young that there shouldn't be such urgency in anything. His mother just wanted him to please her. This made a lot of sense to Joe, as he'd already been doing that. She'd always say he was such a good baby, which he was—no unnecessary crying, or anything, which might upset mama or daddy. This was why instead of the words, "mama" or "daddy," Joe thought that, to make things easier, he'd pick a universal word which pleased everybody. This would be a much more logical thing to do. This word choice he would have to ponder some more after a few more *Superman* cartoons.

* * *

There are many milestones which define people's lives. Adrian and Millie shared a few: moving across the country, getting married, buying a home, and having a baby. After those big ones, there aren't too many others. The death of a parent is a considerable one, definitely memorable, but not one bit joyous, so no one wants to jump there yet.

Babies and young children seem to achieve milestones at a much quicker rate. They learn to crawl, turn over from their backs to their stomachs, talk, walk, and eat on their own. Then, it keeps on going. They go to school, make friends, go to prom, learn to drive, graduate high school, and then head off to college. If your young adult is in good standing, all of these will be completed before they turn a quarter of a century old. Joe was about to reach one of those personal milestones, but not the one Adrian and Millie eagerly waited for.

*The Adventures of Superman* was in the VCR, and Joe was sitting on the living room floor, pointing at his hero. Millie sarcastically thought that "Superman," would be his first word rather than "mama," or "dada;" or perhaps, he thought Superman was his mother or father. It was not like her to think sarcastically, nor was it like her to relieve stress by running to the JC Penney store to shop. Her trip on this day was made possible because Adrian was available to perform the easy task of watching Joe watch *Superman*. It was like being responsible for a small sack of potatoes. Also, on a Friday night she didn't have to worry about Adrian needing at least his 7.5 hours of sleep, which he'd read produced ideal work productivity. Millie announced she was going out for a while, and Superman would have to have his adventures without her.

# Chapter Seven

At JC Penney, Millie was looking to purchase something that would make her feel better about herself, but everything that was "in" this year seemed to have turquoise, or orange, or a nauseous day-glow color. The store looked like someone had vomited in a way and an intensity of colors that could be seen from deep space. She was forced to venture to the section for older to middle-aged women, where there was enough beige and white to make do; but pantsuits would not do the trick. *Christ, I'm still in my twenties*, she thought. It was getting late, and the store's open hours were running out, so visiting another store was out of the question. Plus, her Joe was waiting—not that she felt obliged to return immediately, but she really missed him.

Maybe, if she could not find something to please herself, she could look for something for Joe, and maybe something for Adrian. Not that Adrian longed for new white button-down shirts, which was about all she could purchase for him. He liked to purchase his own khakis, because they had to fit and feel exactly right against his legs, which was fine with Millie. He could do that.

When Adrian shopped for slacks, it was a four hour ordeal. It took only one co-shopping trip for her to let him go and shop without her. She'd also learned that if she tried to shop for him on her own, invariably, there would be a second trip to return the slacks. If there were an exchange involved, Adrian would have to do it; otherwise, there would be a third trip. A white button-down shirt, with a 15.5 inch-neck was the perfectly safe purchase.

So Millie walked into the children's department to find something for Joe. There she found more day-glow clothing, and cheap pairs of plastic sunglasses in those same repulsive colors. She figured day-glow glasses ought to glow in the dark, and they didn't. Millie had the sense not to purchase clothes or shades, knowing that such vibrant colors would overwhelm Joe. Unless he stayed within himself, or found his comfort in containment, he was an unhappy camper. Even when she saw him pressing the warm rocks against himself, she knew he was pushing everything exterior back toward his interior, so he wouldn't feel like he was out of control, or having his inner emotions thrust into a turbulent world. In reality, his feelings of being attacked by outside stimuli were growing as quickly as he was, which caused him to increasingly crave the warmth and predictability of the rocks and pebbles found outside the house.

Millie found a rack of tee-shirts, which made it easy for her to sort past the ones with unsettling colors. Halfway through the push and the grating sound of metal hangers against metal rods, Millie stopped. It felt almost like a miracle, a shirt exactly perfect for Joe. It was perfect like the white button-down, size 15.5 inch neck shirt, was perfect for Adrian. What she saw, almost exactly in the middle of the infant-toddler rack, was a royal blue tee-shirt, with a yellow and red shield-like crest. She held it up, hoped it was big enough, though it looked just a bit small—but without Joe there, she would have to take the risk. In this case it would be just one simple return. Even so, Millie had found the very first Superman shirt for Joe the Superhero.

\* \* \*

This was one of those moments in Joe's life, and one of the first milestones he would remember. An episode of *The Adventures of Superman* had just ended, and Joe sat staring at the screen, enduring the painful intermission before the next episode began. Joe was smack in the middle of imagining the who, what, and where of everything Superman when his mother walked through the door.

"Boy, did I find something that you're going to love," she announced gleefully, placing the shirt onto Joe's lap.

Joe didn't know exactly what to do. *Did they want me to play peek-a-boo*, he asked himself, so he picked up the cloth and placed it over his face. He heard his mother laugh, and say, "He loves it."

*The world is so confusing*, Joe thought, as he deciphered his mother's pleased tone. *What is so different in this blue cloth? Is it some sort of special cloth? Is it the color?* Then his face rubbed against something different in texture which stuck against his cheek. Joe had a fierce reaction, as it felt to him that the sticky Superman symbol on the shirt was going to pull a layer of skin off. He immediately thrust it away from him, but when it landed, symbol up, his heart seemed to burst in magical happiness. Joe let out a shrill squeal, and his mother, immediately grabbed the shirt, and wrestled it over his head.

These few seconds exemplified Joe's chemical make-up where simple items, or actions, often elicited visceral reactions. He had kept everything to himself for his entire short life, and this self-guideline affected him in a couple of ways during this interaction, as Joe had no control over any of the other stimuli. First, there was a delay, from his mother retrieving the thrown shirt, to getting this most wonderful item in the entire world over his head. It was only a few seconds, but for Joe it seemed like the passing time was unbearable. Second, there was the tightness of the shirt. The slightly small shirt's neck was stuck in a tight and painful crown of thorns on his forehead, in a way that most normal people could never know. The action of being dressed in this special shirt seemed to never end timewise, but when the shirt finally popped into place Joe was so overwhelmed by the release of emotions that he smacked Millie in the face. The sound was so loud that the following silence made it feel like the world had stopped spinning on its axis. In that deadly silence, the tightness of the Superman shirt had completely erased the flash of anxiety Joe experienced when he was stuck in the shirt and in pain, and also the shame of striking his mother. Immediately, the shirt became the most comforting and confining entity Joe could experience in his growing world of attacking stimuli. It released such delicious endorphins that Joe was euphoric in the security and safety of it, but just as important, he knew if he ever felt unsafe, he was protected by the most powerful persona possible.

After this unfolded, Millie sat frozen directly in front of Joe, and it was Adrian who reacted. He responded quickly, but in a more aggressive manner than necessary. He moved in like a spastic hawk, and without any sense of grace, scooped Joe up in his arms–as if Joe were on fire and Adrian urgently needed to dump him in some faraway body of water. Normally, this action would have been such an unbearable rush that Joe would not have been able to physically or mentally tolerate it. Now, though, Joe was in such a rush of joy that when Adrian raced him to his crib for a time-out, instead of feeling anxiety, he felt like he was flying. So he made a hissing sound like the one which was played loudly when Superman flew across the TV screen, back in the old black-and-white *Superman* show.

# Chapter Eight

Pulling up to the Gamuts' house in Sunnyslope, Laura hoped that Steven's BMW did not send out too strong a message about her boyfriend. Arriving in his expensive car made her feel uneasy, because she knew the Gamuts drove a Nissan Sentra.

Still, Steven loved everything about his car. It had all the bells and whistles, a high-tech console and the best sound system available. It reeked of extravagance from top to bottom, even down to the comfortable, leather, heated seats–which Laura ragged Steven about because, Arizona was so *freaking hot*. She didn't mean to annoy him, but that was the usual outcome of teasing him. He had been the one to tease her after she lit up a joint on the way over, and then joyfully commented on the BMW's sound system. Except his was less of a teasing tone, and more critical than light spirited. She knew Steven did not approve of her smoking pot in his car—or anywhere in his presence, for that matter.

Laura loved music, but her undersized boom-box at home hardly qualified as a serious player, or even a serious boom-box. The marijuana made the music in the car's brilliant sound system even better, the notes so clean, unbridled, and as wide as the Grand Canyon.

It was Saturday, and Steven hardly wished to spend it visiting a family he'd never met. Laura though, had bought many gifts for Joe. The giant stuffed bunny she had in the back seat was almost as large as she was. When she carried it, it hid her stylish neon yellow, sleeveless blouse and black knee-length skirt. She'd topped off the ensemble with a pair of orange, day-glow sunglasses, which Steven described as the cherry on top of the sundae. She looked exactly the way he wanted her to.

Laura didn't feel like a sundae at all. She felt overdressed, wearing this outfit instead of her casual gear, just to please Steven. The fashionable yellow blouse, combined with her blonde hair color, created such an overabundance of yellow that she felt exposed. She was much more at ease wearing her basic cotton tank-top with cut-off shorts, a look which Steven had originally praised as being sexy, but only when they were first getting to know each other. Then, as a little time passed, she was no longer allowed to dress sexy in any way, but rather, she had to look professional and stylish to satisfy him. Sexy might bring unwanted attention from other men, he warned her, and that could be dangerous. When she tried to make a case against the ridiculousness of that prohibition, even arguing that Arizona was often above one hundred degrees, and that her disapproved-of attire served a function, Steven hung on to his point of view. When she accused him of being jealous and controlling, he just waved it off, almost as if he'd heard it all before.

Being high wasn't helping either. Laura wanted to dig a hole and hide in it. Not that Millie would even care about this, but Laura naturally felt empathy, so she considered everything, internalizing the possible feelings of everyone. The chains she wore for having such empathy grew to be as heavy as ones used to pull up anchors.

Millie answered the door wearing her comfortable Saturday clothes and a big smile, all of which Laura felt slightly envious of. Laura wanted what Millie had—not a baby, but rather, options. She wanted the option to be casual. Steven ruined that option. It was not Laura's fault that she was attractive, as she was certainly used to the attention, and she didn't want to try to control any aspect of that. She just wanted to be Laura, because that had always served her well.

"We come bearing gifts from afar, in Steven's expensive car," her tone switched in mid-sentence, and trailed off from playful to, "Millie, this is Steve." She referred to him nonchalantly, intentionally employing a name she never used.

"*Steven,*" he immediately corrected. "It's nice to meet you. I've heard all kinds of things about your special baby, who Laura is kind of obsessed about," he said apologetically. Laura blushed, and wanted to quickly do something in order to distract herself from this embarrassment. She loved Joe, and found it ironic that Steven called that love an obsession. She noticed Adrian standing over Millie's shoulder, too far away to get past Millie to greet them. It seemed to Laura that Adrian was frowning as well. "He's not classified as special, you know," Adrian countered, obviously misunderstanding what Steven meant.

"No, no," Laura corrected. "Special in a good way... like, amazing special. Unique and amazing special. Just look at him! He is such a handsome baby." Steven shot her a look, annoyed at her for being stoned, but Adrian on the other hand grinned at the description of his son.

"Where is he? I'm dying to see him," she announced.

"Oh, come on inside," Millie said warmly to Laura.

\* \* \*

Mille adored Laura and was grateful to have such company, as her own parents hadn't yet been able to come. Laura and Steven were their first visitors, not including their neighbor, who had left a hit-and-run casserole on their doorstep, and a note, which only said, *from Jane, Your neighbor*. That was okay, as Millie's impression of Jane was she was kind of nosy. She didn't get a good initial impression of Steven either. Millie had hoped that he'd be perfect for Laura, and that when she met him, she would feel the happiness in her fresh, new, relationship. She had wanted Laura and Steven to be perfectly matched like her own parents, who were completely involved with one another, conversing all the time, and even conversing over one another yet hearing everything the other said. If that wasn't to be the case, then she wanted to observe the same yin and yang she had, and cherished, with Adrian; the one where when she moved right, he moved left; when she had the front covered, he had her back. This didn't seem like the case though. Steven seemed uptight and dominating, and she couldn't help thinking that when Laura breathed a peaceful breath, Steven was there to snatch it out of the air.

Millie continued to direct everything to Laura, who had started to dote over Joe, leaving the excluded Steven needing an invitation into their world. When they sat down in the living room, Millie and Laura sat on the sofa, Steven, the armchair; and Adrian stood like he was holding up a mantelpiece. Millie and Laura's conversations were effervescent, almost reminding Millie of how their parents interacted with one another. After five minutes, Adrian sat down on the floor next to Joe and placed a hand on his tiny shoulders. Then he joined him in watching what he later told Millie was his least favorite of all Joe's Superman choices, *The Super Friends* cartoon. Still, it provided Adrian with something to focus on rather than the swirl and bombardment of Millie and Laura's conversation.

Millie thought that Adrian's coping mechanism had been employed well, especially when Laura began to mention a change in career focus, something he would have stressfully internalized, thinking about his own need to change jobs.

"I'm looking at something more interesting than the repetitive routine of the maternity ward," Laura said. "I realized this all because of your son." Steven, across the way, sneered, so Laura added, "and, of course, Steven."

"Because of Joe?" Millie questioned. "How so?"

"I find Joe so interesting, and so intelligent. I find him quite unique. Anyway, I want to know more about children like Joe... how they develop, what are their motivators to enter certain stages of childhood. I mean, I don't want to change any of them. I want to study them, to find out why different babies develop differently."

"But, Joe is just a baby," Millie said warmly. "My little man can't tell you anything."

"That is what I intend to find out. I know it took him longer to cry, and it's taking him longer to talk. You studied Psychology in school, so you know what that means. All of it fascinates me so much. Steven, over there, has been so encouraging. He has an advanced psychology degree. I really want to go back to school, and get involved in children's psychiatric nursing as soon as I possibly can." Millie saw Steven nodding his approval, and felt an unfamiliar irritation rise in herself.

Millie was taken aback by Laura's words because, even though she adored Joe, Laura was saying something which might validate Adrian's fear that there was something different or even wrong with her son. She had worked this through with Adrian, the same ways she had to deal with all his fears—that this was an Adrian problem, not a Joe problem—and what had worked was pointing out that different people do things, learn things, and become things in different ways. Millie would be forced to look for pragmatic solutions to this "Adrian problem," and she had to do it with her solution-seeking husband.

"So, Joe would be like someone's psychological study? As if he..."

"Oh, no, no, no," Laura protested.

"Laura," Millie added. "It is so important that you do what *you* want to be doing. You and Joe are connected to one another for a reason. I'm sure that there will be a lot of children who will benefit from your caring and your insight, if this is what you wish to do."

Millie was grateful that Adrian had totally missed this conversation; he and Joe were too busy, both trying to justify the cartoon Super Friend named Wonder Dog, a dog with no particular powers but with the unexplained ability to speak and to reason.

# Chapter Nine

When the woman in white came to his house, Joe was a little out of sorts. He had been enjoying his Superman shows, in his Superman tee-shirt, actively being himself, then suddenly there she was, and she had changed. The woman in white was now the woman in yellow, which to Joe wasn't a Clark Kent type of transformation, but rather something that needed to be fixed. Joe was just the person to do it; after all, he was Joe the Superhero. Even the woman in white, now in yellow, knew this, as she addressed him directly when she saw him, saying, "Hey, look, it's Superman." In his mind, Joe could outwit or fight off any bad guy, but this transformation hadn't made any sense. He could not control it. *How could she change back–returning with the powerful persona he knew—as the woman in white, instead of being this person in this downright disturbing color, which was affecting him like kryptonite?*

Even though she was causing distress, she seemed to have the same kindness and joy around him as always. His parents also were the same, and seemed to stick to their same scripts of "Say, 'mama'" and "Say, 'dada,'" except this time, immediately instead of merely urging him to answer back, they were complaining to the woman in yellow as well. *Maybe, the woman was there to help him choose which one to say,* Joe thought. He still sought the perfect word to use, which might please everyone. That would be much better—causing less conflict than "mama" or "dada."

Joe backed his logic by considering something he knew—Superman. He thought if only Clark, Jimmy, or Lois could just agree with The Chief, then he would not yell and kick them out of his office. Joe didn't like The Chief too much.

"Why don't you watch Joe for a minute, while I get some lunch ready," Joe's mother said to the woman, in yellow, whom he had known previously as the woman in white. "I think he needs to be changed first."

"Oh, I can do that," Laura answered and laughed. "It's a part of my job description."

"Okay, then."

His mother left the room, and now it was just the four of them, the woman in yellow, talking to him, his silent dad, and an equally silent stranger. It was almost a relief to Joe when Laura scooped him up and they went back to his room and the familiar changing table. She lay him on his back, and gently tapped the plastic emblem on his Superman tee-shirt. "Oh, I like this," she said, then pinched the soft cloth between her fingers.

Joe didn't like what she was wearing, and reached up to try to tug it off her. "Oh, you like my shirt too?" she questioned, gently pushing his hands away. His grip was apparently not as strong as he had imagined it was going to be. "Okay, let go so I can change your *diapey*," she prodded, but Joe reached up and grabbed her yellow shirt again.

"That's *my* shirt," she said cheerfully.

Being alone with her suddenly reminded Joe of the betrayal— the way she'd wanted to use a pushpin in order to hurt him. Joe remembered the betrayal had hurt him much more than a pushpin ever could, and he wanted to avoid it.

"So, are you going to let go of my shirt?" she asked.

Joe wanted to, but he couldn't move. What he really wanted was for her to change her shirt to the correct color. He also wanted to let go of the fabric, but he couldn't.

It also seemed to him that the woman in yellow wanted him to do something too, the same way she wanted him to cry at the hospital. His little hands tightened, as if he were gripping one of his precious stones. His fists were now frozen into a ball of yellow fabric.

"Come on honey, I have to change you. Are you going to let go?"

*Change me?* Joe thought. *I want you to be the one to change.*

Then Joe got another thought. *I will agree to have my diaper changed, if she agrees to change to white clothing. She should know that if I let go, then we have a deal.* Joe's grip instead became tighter and tighter.

Look," she said. "If you let go, we can get changed. Deal?" The use of the word 'we' seemed to fall right in line with his thoughts, which felt amazing to Joe. "Yes," he said aloud, the word thrusting out of him.

She excitedly lifted him and ran out of the room without changing him. Joe was flying again, and he was flying into the kitchen. He began making the hissing sound, the sound which played when Superman flew. "He said, 'yes!'" the woman in yellow shouted ecstatically. "He just said the word, 'yes!'"

Joe knew what he had done. He had found the most perfect and agreeable word in the history of all words, and everybody loved it.

# Chapter Ten

Millie strapped Joe into his car seat and started the twenty minute drive to Phoenix Sky Harbor Airport, to meet the American flight carrying her parents in from Boston, landing at the newish Terminal 3. Air travel was an event which, if everything ran smoothly, Adrian enjoyed the predictability of. The typical flight delays, the baggage wait, and the parking were more fitting for Millie's flexible temperament. For these reasons, she didn't want him along at all. She asked Joe, and he said, "Yes," so that was a very easy decision.

The airport was nicknamed The Farm, as when it was built, it was intentionally placed in a vastly rural area. Millie liked that the city had a lot of nicknames. Joe was born at The Good Sam, her parents were arriving at The Farm, and Sunnyslope was named after the sun on a slope. It made her like Phoenix even more, because in Boston, everything was labeled and referred to historically since its inception.

Joe had been agreeable about coming with Millie, as he was extremely curious about meeting people who were "flying in." The airport, far enough away from home, was perfect if people were flying in. It was safe. Why not have airports in safe, out of the way places, such as farms? Superman grew up on a farm, and certainly he could fly.

At The Farm, Joe instead noticed the big metal monsters which arrived, or left with many people in them. Joe thought that this was pretty convenient for all these people to share flying with each other, even if it wasn't very Superman-like. Still, he was disappointed, as the things didn't look friendly, or safe, and he sensed something quite disturbing about how they might drop from the sky, or crash into rather than leap, over tall buildings at any time. Joe thought it made sense that they landed on long strips rather than jutted in and out of the tall structures as Superman did.

Richard and Samantha Englander were right on time, embracing the greeters, first their daughter, and then Joe. They seemed to have a lot to say, and Joe responded to each one positively with a yes, and a yes, and a yes. *So, you're Joe? We've heard a lot about you. We've heard you say a word or so, but not Mommy or Daddy? It's so nice to meet you?* Yes, yes, yes, and yes, were the responses, and finally, a 'yes,' to *oh, aren't you special?* Joe had successfully managed to please these new important people.

Millie was glad to see her parents. The last time they had been to Phoenix had been during the first trimester of her pregnancy, but she'd felt too sick to keep up with all their comments and conversations, mostly made to one another. It was exhausting to Millie, because in the middle of their tornadoes of verbiage, came conversational pieces, or questions directed to her. Millie was used to it, and could normally follow along, but Adrian became quiet and overwhelmed in the presence of the Englanders. Joe would just respond in the way he knew, and it greatly amused Millie's dad, Richard.

"Ah, so you're a real yes-man," he noticed.

"Yes," Joe responded, which made Richard laugh some more.

"So," Samantha said, "How is Adrian getting on with his job?"

"Legend City is having some troubles, and they are about two weeks behind in their payroll, but we're still doing okay. Adrian, of course, is really nervous about the park going under, but he'll always come out on top of it. He's a solid accountant."

"Perhaps with a more stable company?" Richard interjected.

"Perhaps."

"When we get home, I'll have a talk with him. I have a friend who works at AON Risk Solutions, in Boston and loves it. I brought along his card. He says that AON has offices in Phoenix and all over the world. They even have offices up in The World Trade Center in New York. They are always looking for accountants, to balance their many large accounts. He travels a lot, but the job pays him generously—plus it's a very professional, with a gravely serious setting, which Adrian would love."

The word grave, when associated with AON, for some reason sent a shiver down Millie's spine, but she brushed it off, thinking that, perhaps, the feeling was just nervousness from the oddity of her father addressing her directly, instead of engaging in his usual tête-à-tête with his wife.

"What I mean by grave is that it's more black and white than a western theme park. That's a starter job, and from the sound of it, his starter is close to finishing. It's not a good sign that they're behind on the payroll."

"Yes, you're probably right, but Adrian hates change so much."

"He may be forced to change anyway, and this would give him such stability. I mean, he's nervous about his situation now, and this might be a solution. I'm sure Adrian would appreciate something where he wouldn't have to worry about the basics, such as being paid on time, etc."

"I'm sure you're right, but, let me see the card. I think everyone would feel more comfortable if I approached him."

"Deal," Richard said.

"Yes," Joe said, and Richard laughed hard enough that it echoed loudly throughout the baggage area.

# Chapter Eleven

Millie and Joe were silent in the car, mostly because Richard and Samantha were fully engaged in conversation with one another, complete with the economical use of R and S instead of their full names. On the way back from the airport, Millie noticed that it was always the same dialogue: the Englanders pointing out all the fast-food restaurants in Arizona, which were the same as the fast-food restaurants in Massachusetts. Millie thought it to be odd, since they didn't enjoy fast food. She assessed it as their way of recognizing uniformity in unfamiliar places, to feel safe.

Then they would chat about the weather. Only Richard and Samantha could chat about the weather for twenty minutes. They touched each other's arms a lot during this meteorology blather, and when Joe verbally validated them with a yes answer about how Phoenix was warmer and dryer than Boston, it fueled them even more. Even when they spoke of snow, they turned to Joe, and asked him if he had ever seen snow. His affirmative answer was re-directed to, "he must have seen that on TV," by the Englanders.

Millie felt the conversation she'd had with her dad at The Farm was much more normal than what was going on in the car right now. It was when she was one-on-one with either of them that there was a sense of normal conversation. In her life, each time she was taught major life lessons, the ones which made her a strong independent woman, it was always with one or the other speaking with her, not both of them together. Now that she had been away from her parents for a period of time, she suddenly realized that her parents weren't so enthralled with each other, but rather that they needed to fill the silence, and the empty spaces in their lives, and maybe in their relationship. Why hadn't she noticed this before?

It was right after her parents had discussed the difference in the colors of cars in Phoenix versus the East Coast, and then the effect of road salt on body rust, that they pulled into the driveway of 29 West Sunnyslope Lane. Adrian came out and grabbed their luggage, while Richard began asking how he was, and of course, how his job was going.

"Fine," Adrian said to both, which made Richard want to dig in more after being 'yessed,' for twenty minutes by Joe. But Adrian was already accelerating toward the house with their suitcases.

"We'll have that conversation later, I guess. I've looked into a few things after Millie told me about your concerns with Legend City," Richard yelled at Adrian's back as he vanished into the house.

Millie glared at her father because she was sure he hadn't forgotten that she was supposed to be the one presenting this information. Richard picked up where he left off anyway, when they were all inside.

"We don't have to talk about it right now. When the time is right, ok, Adrian?"

"Fine," he said, stepping away. "Fine."

\* \* \*

Immediately, the usual dynamics of the four adults had begun to take form. Adrian was sure it was fine, and calmer, for him to not be included in their chaotic banter; but, still, it was generally upsetting for him to be excluded, even if he was the one who isolated himself from the rest of the family. Either way, the Englanders unsettled him, as he felt like an invisible foster kid all over again.

Adrian found he was so damned relieved to get into his car on Monday and go to work that he let out a laugh when he pulled out of the driveway. Even with the financial turmoil at Legend City this week, work was a welcome reprieve from all this commotion, and he justified this gladness by thinking Millie could spend time with her parents, and Joe could have a new audience to say, 'yes,' to. This was his time away from all of them. Even the mediocre food at El Sombrero tasted delicious, and was savored longer. The patrons he'd overhear calling the place, redundantly, *The* El Sombrero, didn't bother him as much as usual. A planned audit with the Arizona Treasury Department this week didn't faze him either. He was in such a light-hearted mood today, that the latest sad numbers he pushed at Charles Capel–the park being in the red by $250,000 this quarter–seemed less of a big deal.

"Charles," he said. "Don't worry. It's the dead of summer, and no one wants to be standing in a 110° western-themed desert. Give it another month, and things will pick up."

With everything going the way it was going this week, Adrian was incredibly calm. It was not until Capel brought the architect from the Salt River Agricultural Improvement and Power District Project for a tour of the grounds on Friday of that week that Adrian had an anxiety attack. He knew, after this, and the audit, that his time at Legend City would soon be up.

# Chapter Twelve

Joe liked the visitors. They spoke a lot, and when they asked him to chime in, on cue, with his perfect 'yes' answer to something they said, they would laugh when he delivered it. These people didn't produce much conflict, as of yet, as long as he made them laugh and agreed to everything. Everyone at home seemed to be in a good mood. His mother seemed happy too, even if she had to battle her way into her parents' conversations to get a word in. Joe had never seen that before. His mother always had the speaking role in the house while his father sat back and listened. A lot of what he heard now was his mother having to shout, "Mom, Mom, Mom!" or "Dad, Dad, Dad!" to get her parent's attention so that she could speak. Then, after all the jockeying for conversational points had occurred, they would make plans. They would all go on picnics or to the park together, or go out one-on-one, leaving the third home with Joe.

It wasn't until Friday that Joe processed the older visitors to be his mother's parents. They had left the house earlier, shopping for clothes better suited for the extremely hot Arizona weather. When they came back they were adorned in clothes in the blinding colors of bright turquoise and orange. They even had a green-yellow, glowing, slime-colored, shirt for Joe, "to replace that one he's been wearing for days," he overheard his grandmother say to his mother. His grandmother then entered the room and asked if he wanted to try it on, and, of course, he said 'yes,' though this was not at all what he wanted. First of all, his grandmother was interrupting the watching of *Superman: The Movie*, and second, she was tugging at his tight fitting Superman shirt. Joe began making the flying sound effect, hoping that he would be able to fly away from her. When that didn't work, he began to flop on the carpet like a captured fish struggling to breathe on the deck of a boat. His grandmother was trying to pin him down while calling his name and saying to him, "Why don't you hold still?"

After a few 'yesses,' Joe flopped some more. He had moved, while on his back, from the center of the living room to the edge by the sofa, making flying noises the entire time. His arms were flailing and legs were kicking. He was surprisingly strong for a boy his age. His grandmother, now crawling like a crab, was right on him, trying to grab Joe's arm or leg to get him to stop moving. When she tried to roll up the shirt to take it off, it was so tight that it wouldn't roll easily, so she pulled and tugged, which created such an undesirable sensation for Joe that he flailed his arms even more–and they now were moving completely out of control. Suddenly, Joe struck something, and there was a horrible sound which echoed through the house. It was a loud slap, louder than the hit he'd previously put on his mother, followed by the sound of a snapped twig. He had broken her nose.

Joe's grandmother cried out and rushed out of the room, passing his mother who'd rushed in from the opposite direction. His mother was red-faced, with her stringy brown hair following behind her, like bolts of lightning. Joe again made the hissing sound to fly away, but he was too traumatized to regulate it, and instead of the intended noise, his mouth only produced excess saliva and a strange flubbing sound.

Joe couldn't think. Strange noises were coming out of his mouth, and now the old woman, his mother's mother, who was, a minute ago, trying to torture him, was back in the room, holding the bloody fluorescent shirt to her face. She was screaming louder than the hissing sound he was making. There was so much action, Joe felt he had flown out of his body and was observing the scene from the outside. He saw his still red-faced mother grab her keys and rush out the door with the bloody-faced visitor. The second elder visitor followed and closed the door behind him. A few minutes later, Joe came out of his altered state of consciousness. "Mom, Mom, Mom!" Joe said, but there was no one to hear him. There was no one left in the house but him.

# Chapter Thirteen

Nosy neighbor Jane, after having observed the mass bloody exodus, came by in order to let herself in; after all, her casserole dish was still there. She rang the doorbell, to continue the charade, and not draw undue suspicion. Brushing the hair from her face, she flattened her sundress, looked all around for anyone who might see her, and walked in. She was an odd one, initially leaving a casserole on their doorstep without coming in, and then not coming back to get the dish until she thought the house was empty.

When she saw Joe, she first startled, and called out to anyone who might be home. There was no answer, so she asked Joe if his mom was home, and then immediately after, if his mom was out. She asked if there was anyone home, and then, if he was home alone. Joe said, 'yes,' to all of these questions, so, rather than getting confused, she just thought he was a toddler babbling. She thought she should stay, but also thought she didn't want to get involved. *Nothing like a nosy neighbor*, she thought, and anonymously called the police.

She headed for the front door, but it suddenly opened, and Adrian entered, with a panicked look on his face, needing his wife home to put his prophesied job loss into perspective. Jane was startled; her plan on getting the hell out of there before the police arrived was ruined. "Are you a babysitter?" he asked Jane, thinking Millie never needed child-care, and that she certainly wouldn't utilize a sitter without calling him, especially with her parents in town. "I'm Jane, your neighbor," she said. "I don't think we've met."

"I don't know who you are," he said.

"I'm Jane, your neighbor," she said, "and I—,"

Two police officers arrived in mid-sentence, lights left flashing, as they exited the car.

"I don't know who this person is," Adrian announced to them.

"I'm the neighbor. I'm watching the boy over there."

"I don't know anything about this," Adrian said.

"Okay, okay," one of the police officers said. "We just got a call to check the house as there was a child here without supervision, but he looks pretty safe with all the supervision here." They looked over at Joe, who was standing without moving, his tee-shirt rolled up past his stomach. "He hasn't been here alone, has he?" the cop asked.

"Not that we know of," Jane said, looking over at Adrian.

"I don't know who this is," Adrian responded, as he pointed in Jane's direction.

One of the police officers walked over to Joe and pulled down his Superman shirt, so it covered his stomach. "A little tight, don't you think?" he said accusingly, using the tight tee-shirt to put the fear of calling Child Protective Services into Adrian's head.

"Yes," Joe said.

"Do you want to take that off?" the officer asked.

"Yes," Joe said. The officers looked over to Adrian, who didn't do anything.

With things awkward and silent, Jane interrupted and said, "I'm just here to get my casserole dish. I'd made a casserole for the family months ago, and I'm here to pick up the dish."

"Is this true?" the police officer asked.

"Yes, there was a casserole, but I never knew who made it. We didn't eat it anyway," he added, "we had no idea where it came from."

"I left a note," Jane said.

"Okay, I know this casserole is a big mystery, more suited for our detectives, but I think the situation is quite under control, and we'll be on our way," the cop at the door sarcastically announced.

"I will be on my way too," Jane said, as the police waited a second, and left a few seconds after she did.

\* \* \*

Millie had just arrived at the Emergency Room with her parents when she realized Joe wasn't with them, so she sped home as fast as she could. When she saw the cruiser in her driveway, Millie let out a rare and ugly profanity.

She knew from her studies that leaving a child alone, combined with police action, could mean state involvement. Then she noticed Adrian's car and felt something must have happened for him to call the police. She increased her jaunty-paced walk into a full sprint. Before she reached the open door, a woman wearing a sundress opened the door, followed by the police. *That dress is definitely not police issue,* Millie thought, before realizing it was her intrusive neighbor.

"I'll come back for the dish some other time," Jane said to Millie, as she passed.

"Dish?"

"The casserole dish," one of the officers said to her as they walked past.

It made Millie's head spin. *Were they here because of the missing dish? Did her neighbor call the police because they hadn't returned the dish to her?*

She shut the door. "Why were the cops here? Are we accused of something?" Adrian stood there not speaking, so Millie moved on. "Oh, honey, I had the worst day," she said to him, but he didn't answer. "Adrian!"

Adrian nodded, too overwhelmed to speak. He knew he needed to assume his passive role of listening, without speaking. With her having her worst day, it was not the time to bring up his worst day, which he was ready to explode about.

"Joe hit—," Millie started to say, but was interrupted.

"Legend City is being sold. I'm probably out of a job," Then they stood and looked at each other, neither of them speaking, so instead, Millie began to laugh.

# Chapter Fourteen

By the time Adrian was up to speed at his new job at AON, Joe was about twenty-two-months old. He still wasn't saying much more than 'yes," though occasionally he would mumble something under his breath–but only around his mother and no one else. It made sense to Adrian that he might bond more with his mother, because AON required him to travel one week per month, and logically Joe and Millie were forming a strong union. Still, he had yet to hear Joe's mumblings, and he had doubts that they were actually happening.

Adrian was not a fan of traveling, but it was required of every employee in accounting during the first week of every month. Traveling for a week caused him to feel out of whack for an additional week, each time. The reason AON would float employees to various location cities was for work productivity. Their research had shown that an office would fall slightly behind in their accounting tasks, if employees did the same thing in the same city day in and day out. Floating employees to different cities, with one-week goals, helped them stay mentally fresh. Also, less inner-office bonding helped employees focus on work. Not finishing weekly tasks in a new city was not an option, because if you received three of these "work unfinished" reports in a twelve-month period, you were out the door.

Adrian always finished, even if it meant occasional hundred-hour work weeks, which made him the perfect employee. Whether he was in New York, Los Angeles, Boston, or Atlanta, the cities blended together, without distinction, because the tasks were the same—to input, and diagnose, the green glowing numbers on a computer screen, and to make sure the line-items balanced. It was tedious work, but Adrian thrived. The anxious feelings he had had while at Legend City, where everything, even the accounting books, seemed like an adventure, were gone. Adrian was now completely within his element.

While working out of Phoenix, he would work the numbers on certain accounts he "owned." AON liked having teamwork on these, with the owner being the point person. This person would handle annually meeting with their clients, and completing the paperwork which would be sent to the accounting team, then reviewed by the office managers and geographical floaters. Adrian was the part of the team who handled many of the accounts of the Phoenix Suns. Rick Robey, all 6' 11" of him, would often swing by with game tickets, or framed signed jerseys. Adrian had no interest in those gifts, because ... what did it have to do with Robey's *investments*, or his financial numbers? These giveaways wouldn't give Rick a better interest rate, or earning potential; yet the other AON employees would clamor, accept the gifts, go to the games, and come in the next day with hangovers, and warrior stories.

Adrian never went. He wasn't a basketball fan, which he felt helped him on the business end with the Suns players. During all this, his co-workers nicknamed him Kurt Rambis, a reference he didn't understand at all. It wasn't until he was surfing through his television channels, and happened upon a Suns game on television, that he noticed a few characteristics he and Rambis shared.

Both of them had sandy hair, parted on the side, and Poindexterish glasses. Also, some of the media had nicknamed Rambis "Clark Kent." Factually, though, Adrian was a foot shorter and fifty pounds lighter than Rambis, which he would remind his co-workers, each and every time they referred to him by his nickname. Still, there was a logical outcome to all this. Since he felt he didn't look like Rambis at all, he thought it made his co-workers sound stupid, and elevated his own job status via his intelligence, in comparison with theirs.

Joe, on the other hand, thought Adrian looked like Clark Kent. He would touch the bridge of Adrian's glasses every time he appeared in the living room. At first, Adrian didn't make the connection, thinking that Joe was only imitating what he did to push his glasses snug against the bridge of his nose, a gesture which was observable a few hundred times a day. As Joe grew, and this happened even more often, the action's meaning became obvious, and Adrian wondered how, in Joe's mind, he connected Clark Kent to his hero and role model, Superman? Did he view Clark as the inferior version of a superhero, the lesser version of a man who needed to be changed into something better? Or was Clark someone to behold in his own separate right, as a solid contributor to society? Adrian hoped it was the second, since he built his life around the concrete and correct in everything, just as the numbers he worked on were concrete, and had to be correct. The other options diminished him. He looked down at Joe for a possible answer, but only saw that the side stitching on the shirt Joe was wearing was torn open at the bottom. Upon further review, it hadn't been torn. It had been cut with a scissor, not ripped. Adrian knew that it was Millie who had sliced the shirt's sides so that Joe could fit into something which he was not meant to fit into.

# Chapter Fifteen

Joe thought his mother missed the point about making him feel safe at all times. The tightness of a shirt that squeezed him and held him together helped him to relax, as much as anything in the world. That part was necessary and shouldn't be messed with.

His mother viewed the shirt's Superman logo as its most important element, so she thought that by cutting the sides to give Joe room to grow, she'd keep everything status quo. But Joe was growing anxious about the loose fit, and the randomness of the shirt's flapping against his upper torso. *It's ridiculous that she just can't find another one*, he thought. The shirt's side seams became more and more torn, and once the tear reached up to his armpits, Joe became fussy.

There were other things Joe wanted to disagree about, but his functional use of language, his saying 'yes' to everything, automatically told people the opposite and was, in fact, quite dysfunctional. For example, Joe found different types of fabrics difficult to adjust to, or temperature variations, such as being moved from an air-conditioned car into the tremendous heat of Phoenix. Also, when there were too many lights and sounds occurring at the same time, Joe found it challenging to focus on anything. If his parents were asking him to agree about something during these times, he often flapped his arms wildly to ward them away, unable to say his magic, 'yes,' to eliminate the conflict.

A few days earlier, Joe and his mother had unsuccessfully gone to JC Penney to find a larger version of his shirt, but they were sold out. It happened to be a cool day, so when she placed the torn Superman shirt over a long-sleeved Legend City shirt in the parking lot, the torn shirt flew outward behind Joe. Joe looked like the Superman in the closing credits during *The Adventures of Superman*, when George

Reeves stands in front of an American flag, for truth, justice, and the American way, his Superman cape blowing perfectly behind him. "There," she said to him. "You now have a cape."

Joe felt great about the cape. Physically, it felt good with another tight shirt acting to constrict his body, keeping him in control; and the old shirt, now a cape, met the requirements for still being Superman, and he could continue to feel he was a superhero. When he got home, he stood at attention in the driveway, chest out, back straight, and legs stiff, unmoving. Unfortunately, the breeze had died down, and his cape now sat there, and looked like his mother's stringy hair when it was wet from a shower. He tried to make the flying noise, as if the sound of flying would somehow create the wind and make his shirt-cape move. He stayed that way in the driveway until his mother said, "Come on, Joe. It's time to come inside," to which Joe answered, "Yes."

As he began to walk toward the door, out of the corner of his eye he could see that the cape had begun to move, ever so slightly, synchronized with the steps he was taking. It also felt like the torn shirt's crew neck which anchored his new cape, was too tight around his neck. It was so uncomfortable that he began to run, and as he ran, the new cape began to move directly, as if in flight behind him. Joe, put his arms straight ahead, in flying position; made the hissing sound of flight; and ran as fast as he could, so that the cape stayed as perpendicular to him as possible.

# Chapter Sixteen

Laura started visiting the psychiatric ward at Banner Good Samaritan Hospital during her lunch breaks. She intended to get to know the nurses, form relationships, and then interrogate them about the ins and outs of that job. She told Steven that the ward was too crazy, with more weird people than she preferred, then apologized for using the word 'crazy' and the word 'weird.' The Good Sam didn't have an inpatient children's psychiatric ward yet, but their outpatient psychology departments were known to be excellent for all ages.

Over the next few weeks, Steven did some research. He discovered that she could attend Arizona State University in Tempe, the college from which she had originally received her nursing degree, and switch to a new specialty. He spoke to an admissions officer who said that classwork would be minimal, and she could intern at the Outpatient Psychiatric Center, the same one she had been visiting. This was moving along pretty quickly, he told her.

Laura felt it was moving too quickly. Plus, the internship she was considering was at Phoenix Children's Hospital, not at the too weird, too crazy location at The Good Sam. She thought it was okay to stop by and have lunch inside the psychiatric ward of The Good Sam, and even have lunch with some of their nurses, but the time it would take to even minimally attend classes and have an internship would not be the ideal way to do things. She was working forty-eight hours per week in maternity, just to pay her bills and pay back her student loans.

Steven researched that information as well. Student loans would be put on hold while she attended Arizona State, and she could cut her hours to part-time because her bills would be less after she moved in with him. He had told her all of this over the phone one night, at

11 p.m.

"What?" she said, and stopped sliding the crucifix back and forth on the chain around her neck.

"After you move in here," he said. "There's plenty of space, and I make enough money so you won't have to worry about bills. Plus, I don't want to live without you. I think it would be the best thing for both of us."

Laura hesitated. Her Catholic upbringing rejected this idea of co-habitation, but her own morals concluded that moving in with some-one would be acceptable, as long as marriage was in the plan. But then there was the insinuation that their relationship might be over if she didn't agree.

"I feel this is moving too quickly, Steven," she told him. "And I'm feeling you are rushing me. Let me think a bit."

"I don't know, Laura. What's there to think about? There are no loose ends in my plan."

"I'd have to hide it from my parents. They'd disown me if they found out we were living in sin. Plus, you've already not made a great impression with them."

"Fuck them," he said.

"What!!"

"I mean, you're an adult. You're on your own, and what the hell do you mean by them not liking me?" he asked, his voice rising angrily.

"Stop, yelling!" Laura said, sounding more emotional than she wished. She hated conflict more than anything, and she hated all the petty arguments they'd been having lately. This one wasn't petty though. It was about a real life-changing decision. "My mom thought you were pushy, and my dad thought you acted a little controlling. He didn't like how you butted in, and answered questions for me."

"I did not! Obviously, you're their daughter, I don't stand a chance! They're biased!" Steven protested, as being told to stop yelling only made him louder.

"Well you could have made a better impression, is all," Laura said in a controlled, safe whisper. "Look, I'm not saying 'no' to this, and I'd love to get out of my parents' house. They guilt me so much. I want to think about it, okay love?"

"This is good-bye then," he said, satisfied that she was going to agree with him, but still manipulating the use of 'good-bye' as a dou-ble meaning, to either end the phone call on one hand, or break up with her on the other—instigating worry.

"Good-bye?"

"Yes, I'm going to hang up now. It's getting late. After you think about it some, let me know when you'd like to move in."

After the call, Laura hated how she felt, and she poured herself a glass of wine. She knew she was not a weak woman, but both the choices, of accepting or rejecting his ultimatum, made her feel weak. She didn't want to move in with Steven, but she also didn't want him to leave her. She felt awful for needing him, knowing that his solution to all this was one that actually made the most sense if she wanted to quickly switch her field of nursing and not have to live with her parents. Now, it was 11:50, and there was no chance of quickly falling off to sleep. She needed to process all this, but instead chose to stay up and drink wine with Johnny Carson, so she wouldn't have to think. He had just begun his monologue, and she was intoxicated by the time the first guest appeared on his sofa.

# Chapter Seventeen

Millie sheltered Joe from the world, as much as she could, and kept him as comfortable within his own skin, as *only* she could. This is where flying around the house in his new cape and tee-shirt combo, a shirt which Millie had drawn a Superman symbol on, was allowable, even if it often didn't end well. Joe would fly into the edge of the coffee table, which caused him serious bruising, so Millie removed all tables for safety. The walls and the doorjambs were much more of an issue, as they could not be taken down. Joe involuntarily said "Ow," on contact, instead of 'Yes,' which caused him great stress. Once he struck a door frame so intensely that he had a nasty black eye, and Millie felt uncomfortable leaving the house with him. She'd already learned that her neighbors were pretty nosy about things like this.

Also, Joe now accepted different-feeling shirts, as long as they had Millie's added logo drawn on. Replacement capes were accepted too. And Joe's daily clothes didn't have to be washed every night, as he had clean alternatives to wear each day. Millie was a big fan of using extra detergent and fabric softener, as she liked how her bundles of clothes added a heavy fragrance throughout the 29 West Sunnyslope Lane house. Unfortunately, she had to limit this excessive usage, as the strong aroma seemed to overwhelm Joe. When he put on the clean clothes, he'd immediately roll around on the ground, like a dog, trying to ditch the scent.

Adrian found few of Joe's odd behaviors comparable to those he'd read about in healthy children in the psychology journals he picked up at the library. He thought that Millie should have been the one to pick up on Joe's oddness, as she was the psychology expert in the family, and her failure to do so upset him. The weeks he went away for work were a needed break for him, even if the issues surrounding Joe swirled in his head his entire time away. Joe's behaviors always seemed dramatically worse when he returned. He felt powerless.

One thing he did do, when he traveled to New York, or Chicago, was take the elevator up to the top of their tallest buildings, just to feel, by looking down, that he was at the top of the world. It made him feel in control, yet, if he could do things like this which produced that feeling, why did he feel helpless when it came to his own son? He found he could not adjust quickly upon his return home.

Millie, on the other hand, was fine with all the adjustments she made for Joe. It was Adrian, when he returned, who put stress on the dynamic. She tired of the new, *"why does he do that,"* inquiries regarding everything he observed, and she grew annoyed with him for questioning the things he'd already questioned before he left. She wished he would just be fascinated, the way Laura was, around Joe. Instead it would take Adrian days to get back to his baseline of normal uptightness, which was the norm she could deal with. There was only so much redirection she could do with Adrian, and convincing him that he'd interpreted a situation incorrectly, which he so often did, was impossible. Millie decided that Laura would be good to invite over the first day or so after Adrian came back from his trips. Millie knew that would be a good buffer. When Millie called her, Laura was more than happy for the invite.

"We will come over any time you think is right," she said.

"Oh, just you," Millie corrected, without outright saying that Steven was not invited.

# Part III

# Chapter One

For the next couple of years, Laura would visit once per week. Steven would drop her off and pick her up, as after they moved in together, he'd had her sell her car. He even made a nightly trip to pick up a bottle of wine for her, though she would never tell him that she needed it to feel relaxed in his space. Overall, this arrangement was better than living with, or even visiting, her parents, since she no longer was in their good graces because of this arrangement. She had started her new degree, and Steven paid the tuition. She cut her hours at the maternity ward, working only part-time. These were good things. The bad things were that she and Steven were arguing a lot. The thin gold cross she wore around her neck broke during a fight with Steven; it was snapped, and she never had it replaced. Actually she was the one, not him, who snapped it off when she became upset because he'd said she was better off without her parents and her Catholic upbringing. She felt like a sinner as it was, and worst of all, she was now stuck, reliant on Steven, which was exactly where he wanted her to be.

Steven spoke of marriage often, which would help with her parents, but it made her feel stuck: damned if she got married, and damned if she didn't. If only she could do the things she wanted, then there would be a lot less stress in her relationship with Steven. But that was a threat to him. He feared that if she had too much freedom, she might leave him or have sex with someone else. Laura had determined a long time ago that his fears were not healthy. She was losing friends by attrition, which was only a small piece of losing control of her own life.

*Thank God*, she thought, for her weeklies with Millie. Besides seeing her little buddy Joe, she and Millie commiserated about the status and the strains of their relationships. Millie even told her that

Joe had started to speak in full sentences to her, but only to her. The rest of the world would just get the typical, 'yes' response. *Joe was onto something. It is so easy to just agree,* Laura thought, *and isn't that exactly what I am doing anyway in my own relationship?*

So, she agreed with Millie about Joe speaking, even though she found it hard to believe— because—how could a three-year-old have selective conversations? She had asked about it in her Child Development nursing class, and the professor dismissed it so immediately and harshly, that she thought Millie must be lying. But, then again, Joe had done things differently his entire life, which Laura found miraculous.

When at Millie's, she would ask Joe to say things when all three of them were in the room, or when she was alone with him. After five to ten prompts, Millie would laugh at Laura, and remind her about Joe's selectivity. Millie then mentioned that Adrian had a couple of thoughts on the matter too. The first was that she was lying about it so that he would stop thinking there was something wrong. The second was that there wasn't something wrong with Joe, but there was something wrong with him, Adrian. Perhaps he was so cold as a person, that Joe found him unapproachable. Millie had to remind him that he overthought everything. Millie told Laura that Adrian was pushing for Joe to be evaluated at Phoenix Children's Hospital, which was an idea she was lukewarm about.

"Oh, I heard that Phoenix Children's is excellent. I even wanted to do my student internship there, but I ended up, for convenience, at The Good Sam. I don't think it would hurt to have Joe seen there," she said.

"Oh, I don't know. I think it's just Adrian being fear-based," Millie answered. "Adrian has a lot of fear-based ideas."

"Well, why don't you take Joe there when Adrian is away? After you get back the assessment you can decide what you'd like to do with it, and whether Adrian even has to know."

"Oh, that's kind of sneaky, but I do like the idea of handling it all myself. I mean, it is my area of study."

"I'd like to go, if you want me to, and if you could pick me up," Laura said, then threw in, "It's now in my area of study, as well."

Just then, Joe rushed in wearing his Superman shirt and cape, filling the room with his flying noises. He wanted so much to engage with his friend, Laura, formerly known to him as the woman in white, and then as the woman of various colors, but he was nervous about it; so instead, he flew.

"I'll make the appointment," Millie said.

# Chapter Two

On the morning of Joe's evaluation, his mother was getting him dressed so they could pick up Laura. He was such an attractive and smart boy that she wondered why someone so above the curve in these departments could get dealt such a challenging hand in other areas.

"You want to wear Superman again?" Millie asked, which was part of their morning routine. She would ask that question, and Joe would start by saying 'yes.'

"How about no cape today?"

"Yes, cape. I want to wear cape," was Joe's response to her, the word 'yes' the only word clearly audible within the sentence. Millie felt a strange sense of pride that Joe trusted only her, but hoped that soon all of his words would be equally weighted, and to more people. Still, there was this trust, which proved to her that she was doing the right things. And, why not? Hadn't she changed both the physical and mental environment around Joe to be safe spaces?

"Here's what I think. No cape. I think you'll run around the hospital because of it, and there are a lot of sick children there."

"Cape."

"Joe?"

"I want cape," he insisted, knowing in reality he wanted the protection of being able to transform himself into a superhero, any time he wanted.

"Are you sure?" she asked, and knew she would easily surrender, as there were bigger fish to fry with her son. *Fish?* she thought. *Who catches and fries fish in Phoenix?* The silly little phrase made her miss Boston that much more.

"I want...," he started, then the doorbell rang, interrupting the resolution of their negotiation. "Yes," he finished, in case the person at the door was within listening range.

"Who could that be?" Millie asked.

When she answered the door, Laura stood there in the hot, moist air, but not looking at all wilted from the weather. She wore a white halter top and cut-offs, the color immediately noted by Millie, hopefully indicating fluorescence was on its way out. The casual clothing revealed a fit and confident woman, but it also gave her a look which would turn heads. "Steven insisted on driving me here. I don't know why he has to, but sometimes it is almost as if he has to control even the most stupid things. I think he wanted to make sure I wasn't meeting some guy!" Laura suddenly looked as if she were wilting, and was about burst into tears. She pushed her blonde hair out of her eyes.

"It's okay, honey," Millie said. "It doesn't matter. I'm just glad you're here."

Millie's kindness always helped to lift her spirit, and when Laura bellowed out, "Is the little man here?" her sad, beaten-down voice gained momentum with each word. Joe flew out of his bedroom and into the living room, in his Superman shirt, sans cape. "Are you ready to go?" Laura asked. "Are you ready?" she then repeated with growing glee. "Do you have everything?"

"Yes," Joe said, making a funny face because he wasn't wearing his cape. *Hadn't he told his mother he wanted it today?*

"Are you happy to see me?"

"Yes."

"Let's go!"

"Yes."

Millie interrupted them, "He talked up a storm this morning," she said to Laura as they placed Joe into his car seat for the forty-five minute drive. Without the cape, Joe felt uncomfortable, so he squirmed and vocalized, using his favorite flying noise. It was the only sound which could be heard in the car.

"Not so loud, honey," Millie said. "The radio used to distract him, but it stopped working a few weeks ago and I can no longer drown that out."

Laura nodded. "That's okay. I like it when Joe flies."

Joe's sound became louder and louder as they headed to the hospital. Millie thought it was because Laura had encouraged him, but Joe was only trying his hardest to tell them that his much needed cape had been left at home. There was no backup plan, no extra capes on hand at the hospital in case of emergency.

Millie kept the conversation going. It was her way of keeping the focus off Joe's noise. But the more the women spoke, the louder Joe became.

"I think he's nervous," Laura said.

"Don't worry, honey, the doctor just wants to talk to you for a little bit," Millie said to him after she shushed him. "Nothing to be nervous about."

The temporary quiet was good, as Millie was enjoying her conversation with Laura, which had as little dead-air as the conversations her loving parents had. In fact, without calling each other L and M, the dialogue could have been coming out of the mouths of R and S.

Laura was telling her about a patient she was working with who had legally changed his name from Lindsay Nelson to Shades Creek. He preferred to be called Mr. Shady, a name which did him no favors within the community from a safety point of view, especially since he was scrawny and disheveled. Instead, Shades was often referred to as "that dirty hippie" in his hometown community. Shades also had not told anyone that he needed to be medicated—until he had various episodes and was sectioned to various hospitals. Life seemed to work against him, Laura had concluded.

Shades had moved away from a wooded area of Alabama where, according to his story, they had an annual Salamander Festival. The psychiatric professionals in Alabama thought that he was obsessed with the festival and with salamanders in general, which triggered his mania around the time of their big event. Shades told Laura that he was tired of all the hospitalizations and the harassment in Alabama, so he'd moved far west, to Phoenix, and bought a costume shop in the downtown area. The shop, Barney's Costumes, did well around Halloween but was fairly dormant the rest of the year.

Shades Creek yearned to do something bigger than retail, something which included his love of salamanders, and so, ditching his meds for the first time since his move west, he'd come up with a brilliant idea: An annual Salamander Festival in Phoenix. His first step was to research the lovely critters who resided in Arizona. What Shades discovered was that there was a certain breed of salamander found in the mountain regions of Arizona—the barred tiger salamander (*Ambystoma mavortium*). They were dark, covered in yellow spots, and they grew to be over a foot in length. They also were nocturnal creatures, so Shades decided that, because they were illegal to purchase, he would camp out and capture a few on his own. He stayed up for a week straight hunting them, and continued this practice until his home was packed with barred tiger salamanders. He brought some of the overflow into his shop, where the police thought there might be illegal trading going on. When they came to investigate, they found Shades, who introduced himself as Mr. Shady, naked from the waist up, his chest painted dark brown and black with spots of muddy yellow coloring. The responding officer proclaimed Shades good for admission to The Good Sam, and that's where Laura met him.

"So, what is he going to do once he's stable?"

"His clinical team has encouraged him to start the festival."

"Hunh?"

"Yes, they think a constructive outcome for his troubling obsession would be therapeutic for him, and could create a positive outcome for him and for the community. Then he wouldn't feel harassed."

"Oh, I see. That is a good plan," Millie noted.

"They also suggested he no longer call himself Mr. Shady. Using Shades Creek is much safer."

# Chapter Three

Even without his cape, Joe flew through the lobby of Phoenix Children's Hospital, knocking coffee out of people's hands, causing mothers to pull their children close to their bellies. Millie had forgotten his required cape, and it wasn't until she noticed him running without one, in his current agitated state, that she realized what she (hadn't) done.

"Joe is really upset," she shouted to Laura, across the tumultuous lobby. "I forgot to give him his cape."

Laura moved in for the capture and wrapped him up so they looked like all the others there wrapping their children up for safety. Joe went from a split second of needing to pull some of Laura's long blonde hair out of her head, to a sudden feeling of relief. He enjoyed the tight feeling of Laura's arms across his body, the squeeze he felt from arm to arm. He felt totally relaxed, and Laura sensed this energy shift, and deduced that the cape was more than a comfort totem or security blanket. The cape was something which made him feel safe, almost creating a wall of safety where nothing bad could happen to him, and he could fight for comfort, and protection, like a superhero. She wished she had something similar for herself, some cape, some bubble to emotionally protect her from the so-called important people in her life, like Steven.

When Millie approached, she was out of breath, her loose-fitting, white cotton jersey shapeless as well. "Thank God you are here with us. Adrian would have never have been able to do what you just did. He would just make matters worse, perhaps doubling the damage Joe just did." She left Joe and Laura in their embrace and dropped a twenty dollar bill at the coffee kiosk, apologizing over the din of the crowd, and announcing that whoever lost their coffee because of her son could have a new one.

Joe walked directly in front of Laura, leaving her hunched over in order to keep the needed confinement going. He began to make the hissing sound of flight again because their positioning was quite similar to the one in *Superman: The Movie*, where Superman takes Lois Lane with him on a tour above planet Earth.

But they were not flying above planet Earth. It was Phoenix Children's Hospital, and instead of flying above Metropolis, they were walking down one-hundred-yard hallways which were buffed and shined to a level overwhelming to Joe. Joe's sound, so obvious, made Millie feel something she had never felt before with him. It made her worry that attention was being drawn to them in a negative way. The sound seemed much more palpable on the way to a pediatric neuropsychology appointment, than when it was voiced was within the confines of 29 West Sunnyslope Lane.

\* \* \*

Dr. Ogden was a jolly middle-aged man who must have read somewhere that humor helps in the healing process. Unfortunately, he lacked that trait, and more importantly, it was Ogden's general opinion that the young patients he evaluated were never going to be healed, but rather, that they were to be planned around by their parents, assuming worst case scenarios.

Dr. Ogden was also loud. He spoke in a boisterous voice because he thought loud was funnier, and wore a boisterous Hawaiian shirt, for the same reason. Even his hair, wild and flying around his bald-on-top head, was something one could kind of poke fun at, but wouldn't, because Ogden would always point out his flaws first, in a self-deprecatory way, trying to be funny.

Joe didn't like Dr. Ogden one bit and became noisy himself. When Ogden joked that Millie was the Mexican caretaker, because Laura and Joe were wrapped like a burrito, Joe picked up on his mother's energy and knew that there was something wrong. Ogden even referred to Laura as his mom when he asked her to release Joe into an unfamiliar examination room.

"I am the mother," Millie said in a direct, flat manner, to cover the fact that she was completely furious. "And I'm not Mexican."

"Oh, I knew that. It's just the joke works better if you weren't a gringo, or the mother. Your boy is awfully loud... and you must be...," he turned and said to Laura, lighting up, "Fran Drescher!" Ogden's hands made their way to Laura's bare arm, and gave it a little squeeze.

"No, I'm not the nanny. I happen to be a nurse over at The Good Sam," she sharply answered, refusing to let this middle-aged man even try to flirt with her. Joe was flying loudly against her hip.

"So, this boy comes with a nurse?"

"No, I'm here as a friend," she objected, feeling the word *friend* coming out as not quite the right descriptor. Laura knew she had a large amount of love for Joe, and only hoped that when, or if, she had her own child she would feel as much love for them.

"Well, okay, friend. Could you turn him off, or at least turn down the volume? Does the boy want to come out to play? Come on, son, let's get a look at you."

Laura released her grip and hushed him, but Joe quickly squirmed back into her body.

"Commence burrowing," Ogden shouted, causing Joe to push harder into her mid-section.

"Okay, Joe," his mother said. "Come on out of there and just do what the doctor wants you to, and then we can get out of here."

"Yes," Joe said, and knowing that he had a means of escape, flew out of his confinement and struck Dr. Ogden hard across his face.

# Chapter Four

Weeks later, when Millie received Joe's official evaluation in the mail from Dr. Ogden, she was furious. Most pediatric neuropsychology evaluations for infants or preschoolers take four to six hours. Dr. Ogden had only spent half an hour with Joe, and he'd concluded that Joe's language development was within the bottom one percentile. Ogden had made his conclusions after Millie had told him all the words and sentences Joe could say, but which he hadn't observed. "He's very smart," she'd told Odgen. Apparently, he hadn't believed her, and certainly he didn't take the time to draw anything more than his appalling conclusion.

Joe, also, according to Dr. Ogden, scored very low on the emotional control scale, as he'd received an additional report from hospital security to go along with his fat lip. Ogden also concluded that Joe lacked social functioning, as noted by his observed behavior in the office. The physical shielding he needed from Laura, and the prompting from his mother to participate, helped the doctor draw this conclusion. The only place Joe scored within the average range was attention span. Joe knew if he locked in on Dr. Ogden's questions, Laura's grip would be released, and his plan to leave the hospital, as aggressive as it may have been, could be carried out.

Dr. Ogden obviously didn't believe that Joe was smart. He was unable to conclude, based on the brief observation, that Joe actually had complex coping mechanisms. Rather, he reported that Joe was unable to cope with anything. Millie knew the truth, but it didn't do any good to dispute the findings. She had had enough of people thinking that she lying about Joe, and she was sick of being viewed as an illogical mother, covering up for her son.

The assessment recommended a follow-up with Ogden in a year.

Millie crumbled up the paper knowing that she would not comply with this, nor would she comply with the recommendation to make an appointment with a Child Psychologist at the hospital. *Certainly, not if the child psychologist was recommended by a clown like Dr. Ogden,* she thought.

The final suggestion was for a speech-language therapist. This was one she might consider. If a speech-language therapist could gain Joe's trust, then perhaps Millie might be recognized as truthful—if Joe spoke to the therapist the way he spoke with her. That certainly would ease some of the tension between herself and Adrian, since Joe's lack of verbal range was a growing concern to him, as was her "lying about it." Often, Adrian would call when he was away on business and ask if there were any new words, and Millie was happy to answer that Joe was speaking about cars, trucks, and television shows and asking to listen to music. Millie had always known Joe had a love of music because of how he'd listened when she tried to drown him out during car rides. Now that the radio no longer worked in the Sentra, Joe missed the sound of it. He had made a good association between music and the flying sounds in his head, which to him made both represent escape. When Millie gave Joe a combination of tape deck/radio for his room, Joe would often retreat there after he got his daily dose of Superman. Also in his room was a large array of children's books, which Joe enjoyed. When Millie walked past, she swore he was doing more than looking at the pictures, but she decided to not bring it up. There were other things she needed people to believe he did first.

* * *

Adrian also observed Joe reading, and was impressed. Joe was smart, and Joe could read, learning on his own, really. He concluded this on one of the weeks he was home, and it excited him. Adrian happened to notice Joe intensely looking at a book, at a reading pace, not just flipping the pages as most kids his age would do. When Adrian reported it to Millie, she acted strategically surprised.

Believing that Joe was reading created for Adrian a temporary respite from his frantic fears that his son was so *off* that he would never do anything normally. But it was much more important to Adrian than that. By the time Joe entered first grade, he was already reading at an upper-elementary school level. He read books and magazines about animals, and his favorites were about reptiles, lizards, and salamanders. He wasn't too into reading about snakes, because the fear of poisonous ones had been drilled into his head by Adrian, from the first time he sat outside with his stones.

The hiatus in Adrian's anxiety around Joe was only short-lived. The stock market had a major crash in 1989, so Adrian went into overdrive, trying to control anything he could. He again tried to force Joe to say things to him other than, 'yes.' It seemed that the more he wanted to overcome his inner conflicts, the more conflicts were occurring. The result was that Joe regarded his father as if he were a scratchy and uncomfortable article of clothing. Adrian wanted Joe to love him as much as he loved his mother, and as much as he loved Laura. It didn't seem logical to him that this was not the case.

# Chapter Five

Laura would take Joe out once a week and they would have a picnic lunch, away from the hustle and bustle of the fast-food restaurants most children preferred. Joe was not one of those kids. One time, she took Joe to visit Shades Creek, whom she'd now known for a while. Laura told him that Mr. Creek owned an amazing and cool store, Barney's Costume, located in downtown Phoenix, close to the Business District, on West Jefferson Street. She knew Shades housed salamanders in his store, and salamanders were a particular favorite subject of Joe's reading. Joe initially didn't want to go there, because he thought the store was related to Barney the singing dinosaur. Barney was stupid, and fake, so why would he be interested in purple dinosaur costumes? Joe said, 'yes,' anyway, and Laura took him there. She knew that asking a yes or no question was the way to get him to do whatever she wanted. As they walked in, he saw in the display window the biggest, brightest Superman costume he'd ever seen, and immediately Joe wanted to be big enough to fit into it. It was a *when I grow up, I'm going to* moment. The costume was so new, so bright, that it looked to Joe as if the blue and red colors were magically causing dopamine to explode into his brain.

Joe's own outfit, a faded blue Superman tee-shirt, sized for an older child, maybe twice his five-year-old age, was matched with a red cape made from a bath towel. His mother had found the shirt after *Superman IV, The Quest for Peace* was released three years ago. Millie found it easily available, as the movie bombed at the box office, leaving the shirts overstocked and cheap. So, Millie, at the time, purchased as many of the children's small, medium, and large sizes as she could. The smaller sized ones fit Joe tightly, compressing his senses when he wore them, but he had learned that even the medium-sized shirts, as long as they were not scratchy and had the Superman logo on them, would keep him feeling safe. The large, well, they were boxed in the attic for the future.

Joe, though, was mesmerized by the costume at Barney's. In fact, it was so superior to his ensemble, he couldn't keep his eyes off of it. Even when Laura tried to show Joe the salamanders Mr. Creek kept in his store, Joe had a difficult time focusing on anything but the blue, red, and yellow outfit. Her redirection was futile, as his flying noise was on full throttle, and it effectively blocked out most of Laura's message. It was only after he arrived home, watched the original Superman movie, and went back to his room, that he could focus on Laura's message from hours ago, telling him about salamanders. So he picked up an old *National Geographic* magazine, the one Laura had seen him reading, and reread the article about salamanders in the United States. It created a complete and perfect connection of three things that he liked, Superman, Laura, and reptiles, and young Joe was all about making connections. The biggest one: If only he could wear that real Superman outfit, he would be even more powerful, powerful enough to prevent bigger and badder things from ever happening.

# Chapter Six

By the time Joe started grade school, Laura had completed her specialized nursing program and was fully employed as a psychiatric nurse at The Good Sam. Her day was a lot like Joe's day. There was a lot of documenting and counting of things. For Joe, it was mathematical numbers, and for Laura, medications. For Laura, repetition was the worst part of her job—but getting to know the people who were hospitalized, the best. For Joe, repetition was the best part of school—but interacting with his classmates, the worst.

All the staff who worked at the psychiatric ward loved Laura, an extension of the way the entire universe loved her. Her positive outlook and compassion transferred well. The only person she seemed to have conflict with was Steven. It was almost as if—or a definite possibility that—it wasn't in his best interests to have her happy.

Joe's classmates also loved his positive outlook, and his inability to express anything besides a 'yes' didn't bother them. First graders embraced the fact that the answer to every question was 'yes.' His teacher, Miss Claire London, had been given notice from the school district along with notes from the speech evaluation which had concluded that Joe could only say one word. Anything having to do with the mother's claim that Joe spoke more with her had been retracted by Millie, as she was tired of being called delusional.

Miss London did her best to try to pull vocabulary out of him. She tried word games, songs, even some old theater prompts she remembered from high school. One day she sneaked up behind him, surprising him with a quick question. The result of that tactic was that Joe became so anxious, he had to be sent home, while non-stop hissing like the wind. Miss London knew he was bright; in fact, anything academic or for testing purposes could be assigned to Joe, as he read it and excelled. The simple first grade assignments were so beneath Joe, he'd often escape into his own world, which did, in fact, end up affecting his school work.

Claire London worked with Joe as if he were an egg that could crack at any time, so she stuck with the strategies which helped him to thrive, such as throwing him some vanilla questions to which all the answers were affirmative. "Joe, do sheep eat grass?" and "Joe, the capital of the United States is Washington D.C., yes or no?" It was just for show, because if these were on paper, not only could Joe write down or circle the answers, he could name the types of grass sheep ate in all the different regions of the world. He also could write the capitals of not only fifty states, but dozens of countries.

When the time came for parent-teacher conferences, which for a first grade class normally covered what the teacher really liked about the pupil's personality, Joe's conference was a bit more complicated. Adrian was pretty set that what they were doing was completely in-effective in getting Joe to talk. Miss London told him to not worry, and that Joe was way above the intelligence curve, showing Adrian paper after paper of Joe's school work, certainly at a much higher level than someone in the first grade. "But there is this problem," Adrian insisted. "He's smart, so he should be smart enough to speak." Through all this, Millie gave Adrian various evil eyes, which he never picked up on.

What neither Millie or Adrian could pick up on were the bureau-cratic motives of The Phoenix Board of Education. The board trained their teachers to think that most learning problems are resolved and treated by services that cost money, and that money for these services was non-existent. The board wanted teachers to prove their commit-ment to service by developing a Distinct Education Plan within the student's current classroom, which was, of course, free. Basically, not doing much of anything for Joe wouldn't cost much of anything. "We will continue to use strategies in class to expedite speech in Joe," Claire London, holding the company line, told Adrian. He knew it would likely fail.

"Well, as long as he remains intellectually on top of his game," Millie said, "I'm fine with what's happening." Ms. Claire London exhaled, and smiled.

\* \* \*

Steven also remained intellectually on top of his game, as he remained a reputable, well regarded psychologist. That reputation was stable, and wasn't going to go away. His other problems didn't seem to be going away either. He hated the fact that Laura would suggest strategies for him to not be so controlling, and it felt as if she were pointing out all the faults he really didn't want to confront. He also didn't like that she had maintained a relationship out in the community with former patient, Shades Creek. It seemed unethical to him, and at the same time, threatening. It was difficult for him to track where she was, and he worried she was at places having secret rendezvous. He would tell her that he wasn't jealous, just concerned for her well-being and safety, but Laura knew he was lying, and that her well-being and safety were in better shape "out there" than they were at home. It's not like he hit her, but in the back of her mind, she felt it was possible—that he could at any time. His constant emotional attack was wearing down her defensive shield, an important protective suit she wore while around him, and that contributed to her feelings of being unsafe, and vulnerable.

# Chapter Seven

It was right after Adrian was told by Millie, who was told by Joe, that Joe liked school and thought Miss London treated him well, that Adrian felt the need to, once more, push the communication range of his son. His wife and her friend Laura were out having coffee, and he was alone with Joe. Miss London and Millie never pushed Joe past his comfort zone, but Adrian felt that he needed to do the opposite, and push harder. His son might feel uncomfortable, but he would be there to take care of it. Today was the perfect opportunity to really go for it.

He started asking questions during a video.

"Do you know what Superman was doing, Joe?" he asked, then realized he was dumb to ask such a leading question.

"Yes," Joe said.

"What is he doing, I meant?"

"Yes."

"He is doing yes?"

"Yes."

"Try to answer me. What will you do if something important happens? Will you be able to relay information?"

"Yes."

"Okay, then. Is it possible for the world to spin backwards?" and again he grimaced at the prompting of usual Joe-speak, where the answer is right in front of him.

"Yes."

"How does he do this? You need to try to tell me how he does this." Adrian's voice was getting louder, and the volume now seemed unbearable to Joe.

"Yes."

"Well, tell me!"

But Joe only stood up and did something he never had done before. The running and filling the cape in the wake of his acceleration, was something common, as was the wind-flying sound he was making; but Joe had never left in the middle of a Superman show. He flew to his room, ran to the bookcase, and grabbed a book about the animals of the rain forest. He clicked on his radio, loud enough so he didn't have to hear his father. Then he flopped on the floor and aggressively opened the book. Adrian followed a moment later, stopped at the doorway of Joe's room, and yelled over the music for him to read the book out loud. Adrian thought that reading out loud was a good transition to speaking, and that he was offering encouragement—but instead he seemed to be giving a loud and angry message. Joe did not feel his encouragement, but rather the anger.

Instead of complying, he began to tear his books. The hardcovers he destroyed by their inside pages first, followed by cracking and folding the solid front covers. The paperbacks were ripped, covers first, and then the pages, from beginning to end. Adrian watched as Joe ruined six books; then he moved and positioned himself behind Joe, and tried to restrain him. The ringing in Joe's ears, and the scratchiness of Adrian's presence produced an extreme amount of pain for Joe. He thrust his head back, and split Adrian's lip, which immediately caused blood to run down his chin. Joe's second attempt struck Adrian a little higher, cracking his glasses. Adrian's blue button-down shirt began to collect blood, so he released Joe and headed back into the kitchen to take care of his lip. When the front door opened, the crackling sound of Millie and Laura's shopping bags were drowned out by the long and sustained screaming of Joe, their path to him made easy from the trail of Adrian's blood.

# Chapter Eight

Besides Shades Creek, Laura would see other friends on her days off, and her group of interesting new friends grew with each hospital discharge. This served many purposes. Besides the social interactions she was receiving, she was also doing preventative mental health work. Her favorite was still Shades Creek who, though bat-crazy, was a polite gentleman. Steven felt that Shades had to be hitting on her: after all, how could a man possibly spend time with a beautiful woman without coming on to her? Shades, though, never wanted more than a friendship, never became obsessed, or was inappropriate in any way; and he knew that if he were, their friendship would be over. Laura even watched his costume store while he occasionally took breaks. Not that the store had many customers, but it felt nice for her to feel trusted by someone.

Laura also liked how Shades was planning the Salamander Festival of Phoenix. Shades was doing a lot of research about this. First of all, there were different salamanders in Arizona than in Alabama, so the event had to be planned around that. Shades was doing as much as he could to successfully duplicate Alabama's annual event. It was slow going and still years away from entering the permit process. Laura knew that a complete duplication would be rather dull, so she would suggest fun things which had nothing to do with the scientific and biological aspects of amphibians. Her suggestions were about getting the community involved, having social and family events. She thought of face painting and art, and, for the adults, a salamander-themed dance. She also thought that local restaurants and bars could get involved with special dishes and drinks for the event. It was hard enough, she knew, to honor Arizona's barred tiger salamander, and while involving the entire community would enhance the entire event, it would be an enormous amount of work. Shades nodded that these ideas were all great yet somewhat overwhelming.

The growing years of Laura's relationship with Steven were just as overwhelming, and equally arduous. Steven had more and more difficulty trusting what Laura said she was doing, and with whom. He thought she couldn't possibly be interested in spending so much time with anyone as mentally ill as Shades Creek. So, why would she say she was heading there on her days off? Once, when she was working, he stopped by Barney's Costume and walked around. The place was dark and dusty, and seemingly full of lizards. It was not the kind of place he could see Laura hanging out in, and certainly, the old hippie behind the counter did not look like a threat. Certainly, she must be spending time with another man she was not telling him about. Because of Steven's behavior, Laura had a tough time believing that he was so respected within his field. Steven could act just as insane as her own mental patients.

It helped that she was financially in good standing. She had her own car, which she'd bought with her own money. At first Steven had objected to her owning one, but she knew that this was bullshit, and she didn't have to put up with it. He continued to offer to drive her places, to keep tabs on her, but she told him, "You should not worry about anything if I'm still in this house. If I'm here, it's because I want to be here, not because you have control over everything. Don't make me *not* want to be here."

Increasingly, she found she really didn't want to be there because of his behaviors, so she would spend occasional overnights at her parents' house, after a fight. Her parents were more than happy to see her and to have time to lecture her about her living arrangement. They interrogated her about how it displeased God. The nagging made her not stay there either, but she enjoyed the break from Steven, even though it meant being grilled by him when she returned. She started considering a solution to both those problems—moving in with the Gamuts and out of the house she shared with Steven.

Then, one morning, she woke up and vomited into the sink. She knew exactly what she had to do to please everyone, and unfortunately it was a solution she was less than happy with.

# Chapter Nine

For Laura's parents, Paul and Mary Wellin, pregnancy could only mean one thing. There was going to be a wedding! There had to be, the physical evidence being what it was. No child of theirs was going to go against God and the church during such a noticeable event—a full pregnancy and the birth of a baby. They were still praying to God about forgiving the damage from her last poor decision, so they knew, basically, they'd be out of prayers soon. At least she was back to wearing a cross around her neck, even if it had taken many birthdays and Christmases of giving new necklaces as gifts. If she was not to be forgiven by God, it was still important that everything be in place and look good to the rest of the world. They needed to throw a wedding together as quickly as they could, an idea which was completely agreed upon by their future son-in-law. Finally, they all had something in common. Still, they found it strange that for someone who said they didn't want to be involved in wedding planning, Steven disagreed with Laura's opinion for nearly each decision. It made Paul feel angry enough to think sinful thoughts about biting Steven's head off, but he just smiled and brushed it off, internalizing his angry feelings like a bad case of heartburn. Steven's initial idea happened to be the silliest one of all, suggesting a Vegas wedding, which caused Paul to leave the room before he could act on any of his thoughts. Mary felt that for someone with such advanced degrees, and a successful practice, Steven had no common sense. She was dying to tell him that to his face, but, like Paul, thought it wouldn't be Christian to say what was on her mind.

The Wellins saw that Steven had one advantage. He had enough money to throw at a wedding, and to get things done quickly. Laura's parents would have always opted for the more humble arrangements, but Steven, besides money, had a lot of friends, and with all that money and friends, things fell into place in less than ninety days. Even with having it at a Catholic church, where there was usually a long waiting list, and changing the schedule, Steven had an in. He knew the pastor at St. Mary's Basilica, as a client of his with a sex addiction, so he had something on him which he could use. The pastor held his ground, at first because he knew that patient-client confidentiality existed, working much in the same way priest-penitent privilege did. Then Steven offered a huge donation to the church, but the pastor held his ground once more, citing ethics.

Steven held his ground too. "Not if it's an anonymous tip," Steven said, expediting the decision of St. Mary's Basilica to bump another nuptial service they had previously scheduled.

Steven's ability to get things scheduled quickly earned points in the eyes of Laura's parents, who didn't know exactly how he had pulled it off. The church being secured in such a short time was a God given miracle, they thought. If they had known the facts, their opinion of Steven would have changed very unfavorably.

In comparison, the rest of the planning was pretty easy. Securing the flowers and the food took only two weeks. Having the reception in the back yard of Steven's parents' house, with a small guest list, also kept things simple. Laura had fewer friends than she did six years ago because of her controlling soon-to-be husband. She thought about asking some of her nursing friends, the ones whom she was friendlier with, but then she realized she would have to invite all of her co-workers, to make things right; and that would put the number over their limit. So, she decided on inviting none of them. That would be fine. Her co-workers didn't like Steven anyway, because he was always calling during her shift, interrupting them, to make sure she was there. She then thought about others she might invite. She wrote down her outside-of-work friends, the ones she'd met in the hospital, the Shades Creeks of her life, and then quickly crossed them all out.

She looked down at who might be on her list and realized what she had become in the last six years. Her complete list of invites was her parents, Millie, Adrian, and Joe. Millie would serve as her maid of honor, a singular person in her bridal party. The lined legal pad looked sad with so few names on it, but instead of feeling sad, she felt angry that Steven's manipulations had made her weak. In the past she'd been able to justify the loss of friends only as time going by, and people moving in and out of her life. Now she looked toward herself to blame. It made her look forward to having the baby. A baby would change things, and she could devote her life completely to it, loving it, unconditionally—something Steven could never take away from her.

Paul and Mary took care of buying her wedding dress, even though Steven wanted to go with her, pick it out himself, and pay for it. When it was time to leave for the bridal shop, she decisively told him he was not going, and that Millie was on her way.

The dress she and Millie selected seemed to be whiter than all the others, and when Laura stood in the store trying it on, Millie told her the dress was almost blinding. Blinding the guests might come in handy, she thought, if they saw her growing tummy on the big day. Millie reassured her, telling her, if she was going to show on her wedding day, it would be obvious anyway, and there was nothing that could be done about it. Laura felt satisfied with that answer— yet still hoped no one would see that she was pregnant. Her parents would be so happy if things looked to be in order and appeared morally pure. Not that it mattered much in reality. Her small number of invitees, since they were so close to her, all knew she was going to be a mother; and every single person Steven came in contact with, even the bagger at Albertsons, also already knew, as he had loudly bragged about his upcoming fatherhood to anyone with an ear. Laura thought trying to please everyone was an impossible task, one which made her world full of anxiety.

\* \* \*

The wedding ceremony went off without a hitch, the pastor speaking of their union in the most holy of terms. It was beautiful, and Laura's parents couldn't have been more proud of their daughter. The only issue with the wedding plan was that Steven's parents had tried to pull a fast one on the catering company. They had called their favorite local barbeque place, Hot as Hell BBQ, which had magnificently catered a wedding they'd attended last year. Hot as Hell had built a pit which held a long smoky grill and a giant rotisserie, all wheeled in. Steve's parents wanted the same, but had avoided the usual wedding mark-up by saying it was just for a party. They hadn't become rich without cutting corners.

Before they left for the church, Steven nearly blew a gasket at Hot as Hell BBQ, because they'd parked a rusty old food truck, which had to negotiate its way around back, onto the patch of expensive grass in the backyard. "It's what is brought to parties," the Hot as Hell caterer said, "but, if we had known it was for a wedding...." His parents said they had envisioned the homey environment of a backyard cookout, full of professional cooking apparatus, and all they were seeing was a gray beat-up truck, without a pit, without a rotisserie, and without fancy white chef's outfits.

When they arrived at the reception, after the service, Laura and Millie could not hold back their laughter, seeing the beat-up old truck contrasted against the vivid images of the imagined wedding. They both bent over, hands on their knees, as it was the funniest thing they had seen in quite a while. Then, Laura's face suddenly contorted. Millie saw the immediate concern on Laura's face as she snapped herself up straight.

"Ouch," Laura said, while shaking her head into a slow, 'no.'

"Are you okay?" Millie asked.

"I think I pulled something in my back," Laura said, and leaned back, with her hands on her hips. "It feels a little like a cramp."

"Maybe it's just the heat. Why don't you sit." Millie asked.

"I think that's a good idea. I should rest. I don't want to overdo it."

On her way over to the chair, Laura felt the blood rush out of her face, and she steadied herself to avoid fainting. Then she said to her maid of honor, "I think I'm bleeding," followed directly by, "I'm definitely cramping." A quick denial about what was happening suddenly evaporated right before her eyes.

"Just relax, take it easy," Millie said.

"I think you should call my doctor," Laura said, with hesitation. "The number is inside by the phone."

Millie reached their answering service and waited for the call to be returned. When the doctor called back she asked specific questions Millie couldn't answer without Laura being there. The doctor said they should go to the hospital, but before she could tell Laura, Millie saw her walk past and directly into the bathroom.

\* \* \*

Millie wanted to leave for the hospital immediately, but Laura insisted on staying just long enough to reinforce the air of normalcy, even after knowing what she had discharged into the toilet was the worst thing possible. She would attempt to get through all the first dances, the meal and the cake, and then her plan was to rush off the way brides so often do, as her cover. Millie was the only one besides Laura that knew the truth, and Laura begged her not to tell Steven yet, as it would create unwanted drama at the wedding, in front of her parents. Having this information was hard for Millie. It seemed heavy, especially when she noticed Laura crying during her dance with Steven, and then the one with her father. Adrian whispered in her ear something about showing such emotion, as Millie kept fighting back tears herself. Joe stood nearby, in awe, staring at his woman in white. He looked lumpy, wearing a dress shirt over both his Superman tee-shirt, in the front, and the terrycloth cape in the back. Millie knew that Adrian would have to know the truth about Laura shortly, because she would also be rushing off soon to leave with Laura. She whispered to Adrian what was going to happen, and asked if, after they left, he could announce that Laura wasn't feeling well?

"I don't know. Shouldn't Steven be the one to do that?" he asked.

"He doesn't know yet."

"Why don't you tell—?"

"It's Laura's call," Millie said. "It might be easier for you to tell Steven." Laura was afraid that Steven would upset her parents if he made an honest announcement at the reception about the loss of her baby.

* * *

When it was time to eat, people walked up to the barbeque truck. One of the workers served while the other tallied up the cost of each order. When Millie got up, it gave Laura the chance to tell Steven that Millie was getting her a plate, instead of telling him that she didn't want to move, or to eat anything. Serving the guests one at a time took over an hour, and when Millie returned Laura's cramps were excruciating. Finally, when it was time for cutting the cake, Laura was having a difficult time standing as she and Steven co-held the knife. After the cutting, she sat to be fed by her new husband. Laura had told Steven, when they planned this, that she wanted the cake to be forked into her mouth, without any of the nonsense which was often traditional, and viewed to be funny. Yet, when the time came; Steven smeared the large piece into her face, as the crowd erupted. Laura stood up suddenly, and reached for Millie, seated at the head table a few feet behind them—but she was too dizzy, and she collapsed in front of everyone.

# Part IV

# Chapter One

As Joe became older, moving through elementary school, his life became increasingly difficult. For necessary comfort, he continued wearing the bulky garb of his favorite superhero under his school clothes. This earned him a lot of teasing, and teacher interventions equally divided into those having empathy, and those without. Joe wished they'd stop forcing him to speak, and just let him take written tests, because he aced those. Usually, it took all the way to the end of a school year for his teachers and classmates to accept him at a basic level.

Joe took to being a loner and stayed in his head often. His mother accepted it, and his father understood it. During this time, Joe became fearful of his own outbursts and what could happen if he lost control. He continued to trust in his mother, and continued the need to 'yes,' the rest of the world to death. Often, it was too overwhelming, as people wanted so much. All Joe wanted was his life to run smoothly. Why couldn't he just fade into obscurity, be invisible, or fly away to the upper atmosphere where conflicts would never occur? This would be helpful, because he often felt himself to be in the center of them.

By speaking to his mother when no one else was around, he'd made her his liaison to the outside world. But it was an act that further frustrated everyone else, which made Joe not want to interact with others even more. He was close to trusting Laura, but then what? Even though he loved her, and some of his thoughts could be projected by her, he feared he would be forced into some set of strenuous tests, to speak, to talk, or to communicate with even more people. He remembered the trauma he'd suffered during his speech therapy, caused by not talking, and by the attempts to force him to speak. It made him want to block out anyone in the world who might demand something from him, especially those people and demands which left him vulnerable and feeling like prey. He knew that once he agreed to communicate to the fringe people of the world, he was only going to disappoint them, or worse, leave them wanting more. In his mind, the possibilities of conflict were too numerous to ever let down his guard.

For this reason, Joe felt that if he shunned or blocked others, via his Superman persona, complete with audio sound effects, he would remain in a safe world. Even during school, when the going got rough, the "behaviors," as his Individualized Education Program team noted, would begin. Joe internally questioned the negative use of the word "behaviors," a word which brought conflict within his team, when in fact, his "behaviors" had always been a way to cope with conflicts. When it was suggested that he remove the Superman attire during school, his mother put her foot down, and said now was not the time. Superman would be allowed to be his savior, at least, until junior high school.

Also diminishing his emotional growth were the individual scripts people in his life seemed to follow. These scripts seemed designed to keep him in a safe bubble, preventing incidents. The scripts allowed no demands on him, which made life more difficult when he was outside the bubble, away from the people he trusted. It made the real world hard, and even within the safe bubble, Joe had a difficult time processing information.

On Valentine's Day, David Barker, the principal of his elementary school, encouraged Valentine's Day parties in the classroom, but not students giving out actual valentines. Barker knew that people like Joe might get excluded, and being excluded was the worst feeling in the world, according to the training sessions Mr. Barker and all the teachers were forced to attend every year, thanks to the Board of Education. Of course, there were always parents who formed and acted upon their own strong and noble beliefs about paper valentines. These parents were the ones Barker considered to be pains in the ass, something he learned directly through firsthand experience, and not through a required training session.

Joe's mother, one of those who ignored the memo, wanted Joe to give his all classmates valentines. She thought it might be an acceptable way for Joe to socialize without having to talk. Joe didn't

want to do this, so he kept the pink, red, and white cards in his backpack. Millie understood why he returned with the backpack full of the
cards. What she didn't understand was why there was one missing.

There was one other girl, Grace O'Halloran, who agreed with her
parents' decision to overrule the principal, and thought it was a good
idea to give all the boys in her class valentines. The O'Hallorans
viewed giving valentines as a sweet and friendly gesture, which
should be allowed. Grace was a brash, popular, and certainly confident girl, who enjoyed attention from the boys. She also had been
taught firm stances for girls against gender role stereotypes and power
structures, so she figured that giving out valentines was empowering.
When it was time for Grace to give Joe his, she paused. Here was a
boy, who was cute, but quite different from any of the boys she knew
in class. He never gave her the attention the other boys did, which
she liked and felt challenged by. He seemed to have better things to
do. So she pushed the issue.

"Do you like me, Joe, because I might like you," she said, trying
to get him to notice her. Grace was very noticeable. She had auburn
hair, which was thick and the texture of silk. She also had started to
develop by the sixth grade, which was something the boys noticed as
well.

"Yes," Joe said, as he accepted her bright red envelope. Then he
walked to his backpack and gave her the only Valentine's Day card
he would give to anyone.

# Chapter Two

Adrian's new company, AON put the employees and their families up at the Four Seasons, Los Angeles, at Beverly Hills in order to motivate them. Adrian felt it was similar to the benefit offered at Legend City, which were free passes to the theme park. It was AON management's idea for the employees to bring their families too, and have easy access to some of Hollywood's premier attractions. Not that this mattered, as Joe would rather stay indoors, causing him and Millie both to stay inside the hotel. Adrian imagined Joe was a Hollywood movie star, a public icon, who never felt at peace when out in public.

To Adrian, Hollywood was indeed similar to Legend City, a created place which felt fake. Adrian, like the rest of his family, didn't want to venture too far, as the hotel had all he needed. The room had a bed, a bureau, a closet, cable television, just like any other work hotel he stayed at. He might as well have been in Kansas City, Missouri, or West Des Moines, Iowa, because they had all those amenities as well. Adrian felt obligated to accept AON's reward, but internally questioned how this could be a treat for him. It had many drawbacks, as the Four Seasons was five miles away from the office he was auditing, and it took almost thirty minutes to get there. Also, the tourist junk had no significance to him. Hollywood was filled with a group of people who worked in movies, and television, which seemed to be logically equivalent to his AON co-worker group, the sense being that Hollywood people and his co-workers all were employed. The difference was that no one was traveling to Phoenix to gawk at AON offices, or paying for a tour to drive past his house in Sunnyslope, Arizona.

Adrian tried to reason that his son, too, was like anyone else. He went to school, he studied, he passed in his homework, which was all good. On the flip side, Joe didn't seem to make connections with anyone, except with Millie, and perhaps some, but less, with Laura. He also remembered some phenomena Millie was studying about the time they were first dating, something known as the Observer Effect. It was one of the reasons he first connected with Millie, because it was a theory both psychological and measurable. God, he remembered how they had spoken about this for hours back in Tower C, in Boston, the basic example being the temperature of a thermometer affecting the temperature of the solution being measured. At the time, Adrian had difficulty grasping the examples which involved people, because people could be unpredictable. He thought more about adding a 125 degree Farenheit thermometer to a 50 degree Farenheit ounce of water.

He now understood that his son was not at all affected or shaped by others, but rather, completely overcome by outside stimulus. Others were influenced by the outside stimuli of the world, but Joe, on the other hand, was trying to use himself to change the outcome of the world itself. Adrian's conclusion could only be that it was impossible to see Joe's part of the Observer Effect if the observer only wanted to stay hidden.

When he got back to the hotel, later that night, he brought this up for discussion. Millie disagreed with this idea, in theory. After all, wasn't she influenced by Joe's idiosyncrasies, and, for example, was stuck inside at The Four Seasons because of Joe? Wasn't she stuck 24-7 with him the rest of the time too? She pointed out that the theory was psychologically sound, but it didn't take into account why Joe chooses who to interact, or not interact, with. They bickered about it for a few minutes, until Adrian backed down and agreed with her logic, just to smooth things over. This was more within her area of expertise, he reasoned, and unless there were numbers to balance, he should continue to let her be responsible for a child she had, as she mentioned, *nearly all the fucking time.*

# Chapter Three

Millie's frustration about feeling trapped continued, but she knew that she was the best person to be there for Joe. She even mentally bought into the superhero concept, both with his obsession, and now her own feeling that she was a superhero in her role as caretaker. The last person she wanted to be was a martyr as it was against everything she had learned in life. Strong women were not martyrs, and just as she stressed independence to Laura in regards to Laura's relationship with Steven, she had something to work on with her own independence in her life. The mantra she held in her head was in the combined voice of her parents, Richard and Samantha; she heard over and over, *independence sets women free.*

But for independence she knew she would have battles of time management. Joe was currently in elementary school, soon to be in junior high school, and before she knew where the time went he would be graduating high school. Then what? For the sake of her own life, she had to push Joe to be the most independent person he could be; otherwise he would never be prepared, even as he grew to adulthood, to leave her side. Thank God, Joe was smart. Those who didn't know him, such as outsiders, assumed that since he didn't speak much, this wasn't the case. Millie knew better, and worked on him to excel at such things as balancing her checkbook, working the family budget sheet, writing checks, and sending out the bills when they came in. The inadvertent side effect of this was the complete approval Joe was receiving from his father for mastering these tasks.

Millie also gave him shopping list worksheets. Joe would calculate the amount of food to buy for each family meal, and then proportionately change the amounts of food as if he were only purchasing to cook for himself–Millie's eventual goal for him. Joe even had boxes of cereal purchased just for his use, so he could gain knowledge about how many ounces of cereal per week he would consume, and then, the estimated time it would take before he'd have to replenish the stock.

Millie knew the most difficult training was yet to come. It didn't involve measurable concepts, but rather desensitizing him to the outside sights, sounds, fabrics, and language which overwhelmed him and caused emotional breakdowns, which led to complete anthropophobia. She knew her first and most difficult task would be replacing his use of shirt and cape and somehow having him mentally accept that, so he could look normal while feeling safe and protected. The use of a towel tied around his neck just wouldn't fly in society. Coincidentally, *fly in society*, was the same phrase Adrian recently used unintentionally, and then didn't understand why Millie laughed. When she repeated it back to him, he just stared at her blankly. It was the stare she often saw in Joe after she suggested such things as, "Joe, soon you will be going to Albertsons to shop for us on your own"—the stare which was soon followed by his Superman flying noise. Millie knew that she was going to need some help to find out what to do about *that*.

# Chapter Four

After her marriage and the loss of her baby, Laura needed the Gamuts and her outside friends, more than ever. The wedding made her feel tricked. It was as if Steven had gotten her pregnant then taken the baby out of her, so that he would be locked in. At first, he was kind and sympathetic about the miscarriage. This lasted about a week. Then it was back to normal, with the addition of him demanding that she snap out of her depression. He even threw out the flowers that had been sent her, before they had died.

"Although the world is full of suffering, it is also full of the over-coming of it," he argued. "Think about Helen Keller." For someone in the world of psychology, his treatment of this traumatic event, one he was directly involved in, defied logic.

"Fuck you," she said.

She took a few weeks off working in the psychiatric ward and helped out at Barney's Costumes, partly to get out of her head, but mostly, to avoid being at home or in a hospital-like setting. If she'd still worked in maternity with all the babies, she would have quit outright. It helped that Shades Creek was thrilled to have her at Barney's, using this time to fine tune his plans for the initial Salamander Festival.

Laura's strategy of involving the community had been a god-send. First, Shades focused on getting the small businesses involved, and once they had committed, the larger ones could be approached. Souper Salad got wind of the festival and immediately aligned itself to the proposed event. The Regional Manager felt it was the perfect promotional opportunity, and imagined a salamander eating leafy greens on banners all over Phoenix.

Shades knew salamanders were extremely carnivorous. They

readily ate maggots, mysis, springtails, buffalo worms, fruit-flies, and crickets, none of which would be good for Super Salad's business banners. Shades knew that no restaurant would want to be associated with the real diet of the salamander, especially the maggot part. "They can do whatever they want with their own belief system, make their own banners, just as long as they buy in," Laura told Shades. Souper Salad agreed to give a big hunk of sponsorship money to the festival, and Shades didn't correct the company's incorrect beliefs.

Besides Shades Creek, Laura also spent more time with Joe, helping him adapt to his increased independence, while following Millie's script. She tutored him in budgeting, using a fictitious budget, with Joe purchasing enough food at Albertsons, with the given dollar amount to last him for a week. Joe often had to be reminded that the exercise involved shopping for himself, and himself only, because if he thought about adding in his mother and his father, he'd go over the budget every time. Laura didn't like the fact that his mother would always prompt him with, "What would happen if we weren't around?" because she worried that Joe would become upset. She also strategized that Joe needed to complete the training by actually going to Albertsons, and he would most likely succeed, shopping at the times the store was less busy. It was too bad she slept at 3 a.m., as Albertsons was open twenty-four hours, and that would be a good teaching time for Joe.

"Where have you been?" Steven would ask when she returned, but her answer never mattered. He was always convinced she was having an affair.

*I might as well be,* Laura thought. *I get treated as if I were anyway.*

# Chapter Five

Joe didn't want to attend his elementary school graduation, as too many things could go unpredictably wrong, but his mother made him go. Millie felt that even something as stupid as a sixth grade graduation was a chance for Joe to fit in with his classmates. When he walked up to the podium to accept his diploma from Principal Barker, he froze. He wished his mother could be up there with him, as she made him feel safe through what he perceived to be random moments. At the diploma exchange he and Principal Barker got involved in Joe's one-word conversational script, which often influenced the direction of any interaction.

"Congratulations," Principal Barker said.

"Yes," Joe said.

"Come on, Joe, take it," Barker urged, smile plastered on his face.

"Yes," Joe said.

"Here you go."

"Yes."

"Are you going to take it?"

"Yes."

Principal Barker was on the microphone the entire time, so the situation was made worse as their interaction was broadcast over the P.A. system. In the bleachers, a *what is wrong with that boy* uttered by a parent, was loud enough to be heard without a P.A. system.

Joe thought that punching Principal Barker would be a good way to gain possession of the diploma. Wasn't that the end game? Then something amazing happened. His classmates started chanting, "Yes, Superman, yes," to encourage him to take the diploma. Joe thought those 'yesses" were the entire school wishing for him punch Principal

Barker in the face, to end the standoff. After another few seconds, which seemed like an hour to him, Joe balled his fist.

Behind him, waiting impatiently to get her diploma, complete with the anticipated loud cheers, was Grace O'Halloran. Ever since Valentine's Day, Grace had paid a lot of attention to Joe, more than anyone else in a class which only knew Joe as the boy who said 'yes' all the time. Unlike them, she was quite keen in understanding his behavior. She knew he was unique, and tried to understand why. After all, he had said 'yes' to liking her, something which she knew, based on experience, only certain boys were brave enough to be open about.

On the podium, she saw Joe's fists cocked, so she raced up and accepted the diploma for him, and placed it in his hands. "It's okay, Joe. You can go now," she said, the interaction heard over the microphone. Grace's act of kindness was mistaken as something else, because the crowd laughed at her perceived impatience, not showing any sign or appreciation for what had actually just occurred. Millie understood, and–thank God–Adrian was out of town, as Grace's act probably would have embarrassed him.

# Chapter Six

Millie wasn't embarrassed, she was grateful. After the ceremony, she went out of her way to thank Grace and compliment her parents on their childrearing. "That's okay," Grace said, "Joe's cool. Besides, you know, he's really handsome, and smart. He just gets stuck sometimes." The O'Hallorans proudly complimented their daughter as well.

Millie would dream later that night of Grace asking Joe about what was going on in his head, and Joe, fully trusting her, answering her questions in complete sentences. Grace would take notes using pad and paper so that she would not forget a single word. Then, Joe would invite her to fly over Phoenix, her luxurious hair flowing in the wind... and yes, Millie thought, *I have seen that movie thousands of times too.*

Her husband, of course, was always worried about what would come next. What will happen when Joe enters the new school, and the narrow pieces of acceptance he had earned were completely wiped away? What will happen if the good kids like Grace decide that Joe is no longer cool, with his cape and tee-shirt? Joe might not gain acceptance at Madison Meadows Junior High School, and kids could be pretty cruel about it. He pictured the bullies, ripping the tee-shirt and cape off him, and then stuffing Joe in a locker.

Also, there would be Joe's file that would be transported to the new school. Though it would probably not be read, it would cause Millie to have to *train* the new teachers, at some point in early September. In the new and larger school, there would be more teachers to train. In elementary school, Joe had one teacher each year, and even with that, it took nearly a full year for the teacher to get in sync with the strategies he or she needed to use with Joe. Joe would now have six teachers, with seven classroom transitions per day, including lunch. Millie wished she could chaperone Joe around the school next year, but that certainly wouldn't be too cool either. Then, of course she later dreamed that she was being stuffed into a locker, wedged in next to Joe in the dark.

Then there were new social situations which Joe would be incapable of participating in. 'Yes,' would only go so far. Joe would be twelve, and there would be the interactions between boys and girls with surging hormones. How would Joe fit into that? Would Grace be disappearing as a bridge for Joe with all the other kids? There were so many questions to consider, and try to solve, with the summer vacation only a few months long.

Joe would embrace this break from school. He would dive into his world of books, music, and television. His agitation seemed to be worsening, though, whenever Millie or Laura suggested leaving this safe place. His 'yesses' were quicker, blunter, and often Joe would throw the word out before the question had even been finished. Millie felt that the older he became, the more he attempted to avoid. Even his conversations with Millie were fewer, less detailed, and farther between. He couldn't hide as well behind his Superman outfit, as Millie had him wear the Superman shirt under another, and was using a scissor to slowly reduce the size of his cape. She took a few quarter inches at a time, every other day. Joe tried to confront Millie, regarding his lessening cape, using a single sentence, and Millie explained the reasoning behind it, which Joe agreed with. Conflict-wise, this was the thing to do, and logically he understood the need to fit in at a new school, but the shorter the cape became, the more it felt as if cape was like a fuse burning, becoming shorter as it headed toward a stick of dynamite.

# Chapter Seven

Joe realized that starting school was a big deal, and it was big especially because everyone else was making a lot of noise about it. In between the noise and advice, Joe's brain was working in overdrive, trying to figure it all out. There were the other kids, who were clueless. Didn't they realize how hard it was for him to avoid conflict? They must have something wrong with them as they were the ones causing conflict each and every day. Every... single... day. Joe's worries built up. They were included in his unresolved list: the cape, the tee-shirt, the kids, the school, the teachers, the classes, the speaking, the adjustment, and all the other unknowns, et cetera, et cetera, et cetera. His anxieties were a blur, all spinning around in his head, like a carnival wheel. If only someone would make the wheel stop, instead of spinning it over and over again. Joe made a concerted effort to put his mind in major flight over Sunnyslope, over the city, and away from the universe.

Joe enjoyed this fantasy world. There was no conflict in it, and if people tried to take him out of it, he would say "yes." All his increased escapism didn't go unnoticed by his parents. It was his mother especially who continued to interfere with the safe and pleasant thoughts he *needed* in order to get away from the unpleasant pieces of the world. In some cases his mother was one of the unpleasant pieces. Often she would push without understanding the full picture. For example, when he went swimming and the air was cooler than the water, the change in temperature felt like an electric shock which covered his skin. His mother thought the reason he didn't come out of the water was because he liked swimming so much. She couldn't understand the pain, as she couldn't feel it. He could be Superman all he wanted, but that wouldn't help. Even his avoidance tactics, like imagining flying through the air, couldn't cut the pain of a billion pin pricks poking his skin simultaneously.

The one thing Joe would do was go with Laura to Barney's Costumes; but he would not enter. He was happy to stand outside, and look through the window at the Superman suit. Laura used to try to get him into the store, but she had given up, so while Joe stared at the suit, Laura used the time to check in with Shades. She left him outside by the window, totally engrossed. It was something for Joe to be positive about, especially with his own suit getting cut shorter by the day. His cape and tee-shirt facsimile felt bogus compared to this amazing, bright, new suit, which felt mystical. It was so marvelous that he believed if he wore it, something magical would probably happen and he really would legitimately fly. Christopher Reeve, now paralyzed, couldn't make movies anymore after he had an accident as a mortal; so it had to be the suit, he reasoned. It had to be. Joe felt this suit would fix what was wrong and unsafe in the world, including what was wrong with him.

# Chapter Eight

*How can I help him?* Millie asked herself. It would be so much easier if the world accepted Joe on Joe's terms, as there were so many things he did well, and from the naked eye he looked like everyone else. *Yes, he gets overwhelmed, and yes, he only says 'yes,' to most people. 'Yes,'* she thought, *'yes, yes, yes.'*

Millie observed that Joe was becoming more anxious around the reduction of his cape and was speaking less to her. He was getting too big to act out on his anxiety, make his block-out noises or run around the house. These behaviors couldn't be overlooked anymore because of his age. Millie felt that it was her responsibility to help Joe accept himself on his own terms because, with that acceptance, and with Joe being less stressed, he might find more approval from the rest of the world. She feared that this might be difficult because of her own past denial of the things which were wrong with him, her habit of making them less significant in her own mind than they actually were.

So the cape cutting stopped after Millie gathered up all the capes, washed them, and for one last time, cut them small enough to run half-way down his back, under another shirt. Millie thought she could explain it to others as protection against sensitive skin. If she explained it that way, would it still be viewed as weird? Perhaps if Laura wrote a note on the Psychiatric Ward's letterhead...?

*God.*

Millie knew that whoever read it would find both the note and the letterhead weird. His IEP read that the cape and tee-shirt were viewed as "role-playing," but, as noted by the team at his elementary school, it was something not recommended to be carried over to junior high school.

*That's all fine and dandy,* Millie thought, *and easy. How easy it was for that team to recommend something that they were unable to carry out on their own when they were the teachers.* If the cape were hidden well enough, and the Superman tee-shirt worn under another shirt, maybe it might be socially acceptable. Millie knew it would only be a matter of time before she would receive a phone call, in which she would have to defend the cape and tee-shirt as necessary, to a school administrator. It seemed it was she and Joe against the world. She wished Adrian were part of the fight too. He, in his own way, attempted to do something which might be a teachable moment for Joe. During *The Quest for Peace* tee-shirt shopping for Joe, Millie had bought a blue Superman necktie for Adrian, as something Joe could give him on Father's Day. Adrian never wore it anymore as, according to him, it was not appropriate for the seriousness of the work he performed. The truth was, at the time, Adrian was trying to dissuade his co-workers from making their Kurt Rambis-Clark Kent comparisons; and if the tie made his co-workers think of Superman, then wouldn't that counteract his attempt? He didn't know because the question fit under psychology and not logic.

Then, one day, a week before school started, Millie noticed Adrian wearing a royal blue suit he had bought on his last work trip to California; it matched the Superman necktie he was also wearing— perfectly. Millie knew exactly how his mind worked, and although she thought what he was doing was a reach, she felt very endeared to him by his attempt. Adrian was trying to show Joe a more socially acceptable way to wear the outfits he wanted. Again, his logic didn't stand a chance because as Joe saw it, a Superman logo on a guy who had to push his glasses up against his nose constantly, and was obviously not Superman, made no sense whatsoever.

# Chapter Nine

Every entity has a rule, a measure, likelihood, or prospect of something still to come. The key to getting through life is to figure out all those things, within the boundaries of the setting you find yourself in. This is the exact reason why Adrian was wearing the blue suit and Superman tie combination. It was also the reason he discarded that outfit before he entered the Phoenix office and changed back into it before he returned to Sunnyslope. He might wear the suit if he were out on a business trip in California, or Europe, but certainly not the tie. He'd learned all that from his attempted transformation away from Kurt Rambis.

Adrian was traveling more and more, and adhered more and more to rules for each location. It was all getting pretty easy for him, as he'd been at AON for around ten years, and Kurt Rambis had just retired from the NBA. His co-workers seemed to be jumping ship frequently enough for him to have a lot of seniority at AON, so Kurk Rambis seemed to lose value as a reference. With this seniority, he didn't have to travel as much; but the truth was, it felt good to be away from home.

Being away fit his personality. Adrian would arrive at the satellite offices early, and leave late. Often, he was the first in, before the regular staff arrived. He had the sign-in keys for each office, and he audited what needed to be audited, and fixed whatever needed to be fixed, without any distractions. Most of his Phoenix team would use their time away to go out late and hit their favorite bars. They'd arrive late to the office the next morning, hungover and inefficient. Often numbers were missed, their spreadsheets left unaudited; and their overall recovery was only found, with the hair of the dog, later that night. Adrian, on the flip side, was all business and had become so efficient at his job that he was able to review, and fix, all of his co-worker's errors and review any of their ignored spreadsheets. He was extremely well respected by his AON team, because his hard work covered everyone's asses.

At home, it was quite different, as Adrian's home was stressful, with both Millie and Joe igniting his worry, like a match on flint. His hotel rooms were always the same brand and same location. He could watch CNN in each, and this was the most peace he had in his life. With him and Joe, he felt like they were opposite electrical charges interacting, with Joe having a much stronger magnetic field than he did. It forced him to feel repelled, not having as much influence as a father normally would on his son. Thank God for Millie, because she was good at what he was not good at, but still, the feelings of closeness that they used to share as husband and wife, were now chock full of resentments. Millie reported the goings on upon his return from a trip, the same way anchor people on CNN would flatly read the news, or even a light human interest story.

Adrian thought their marriage was in a rough patch, and they needed to work on it, but like Joe, Adrian was an expert on avoidance, even if it weren't as obvious. Adrian had a hunch that his wife might suggest marriage counseling, but feared that Millie, with her degree, would run roughshod over him. And, according to statistical studies, there were high percentages of divorce rates for those who went through counseling together. In some cases, marriage counseling worked by convincing a couple that they are not in a healthy relationship and by encouraging the couple to think they are strong enough to end their relationship. According to what Adrian read, approximately a quarter of couples who receive marriage therapy reported that their relationship was worse two years after ending therapy, and up to 38% of couples who receive marriage therapy got divorced within four years of completing therapy. Adrian also found in his research that for around 30% of the couples coming into marriage counseling, divorce was already on the table for one of the parties. Traditional marriage counseling has no way to deal with that type of person. Adrian thought that it was a positive sign that a request to attend counseling hadn't been suggested yet, since, according to the numbers, divorce wasn't currently being considered by his wife, at that high rate where counselors had no power to do anything about it. Adrian was 100% certain that he wanted to stay in his marriage.

# Chapter Ten

Laura too, in her marriage, had become great at avoidance, which made her feel guilty when she gave advice to Millie about her issues with Adrian's avoidance. After these conversations, Laura would go back home and try to be as considerate and kind to Steven as possible. Then, she felt terrible for pandering to him, an unsupportive asshole. Millie, who was all for women being strong enough to leave a bad marriage, seemed somehow hypocritical when it came to describing her own relationship. After all, in her case, Adrian's problems were beyond his, or anyone else's, control, and one problem they *could* control was how they should both deal with their son, Joe.

Laura often thought of how different her marriage would have been if her baby had been carried to full term; and although her co-workers had encouraged her to "try again," the last thing she wanted was to be intimate with Steven. It repelled her when he reached for her at night, and if it went anywhere further than a goodnight kiss, such as him fondling her breasts, she recoiled as if he were burning her. Being considerate and kind was one thing, but Laura felt no obligation to be the "good wife," who closes her eyes and dutifully waits for her husband to finish. It seemed an entire lifetime had gone by since he first approached her, at the movie theater, on that evening twelve years ago.

Laura also was becoming more and more annoyed with her husband's growing jealousy over Shades Creek. She was just tired of defending herself regarding the uncombed, dentally challenged, Shades. To think that she might be having an affair with him, which is what Steven continued to fish for, was ridiculous; but it still formed a disturbing image in her head of her and Shades together. She *was* excited that Shades was actually getting The Salamander Festival of Phoenix,

Arizona, off the ground. He really thrived when he was in his near-manic state, as he could accomplish a lot; but he needed Laura's expertise to keep his energy well-balanced. For example, Shades had petitioned that the festival take place at the Hance Dog Park, located in the smaller northeast section of Margaret T. Hance Park. Shades reasoned that since dogs and salamanders were both animals, the leap from dog lover to salamander lover would be an easy one for the general animal lover. Laura's training allowed strategic redirection, without conflict, to successfully shoot down the flawed logic of Shades Creek. Laura told him that the dogs themselves wouldn't be interested in a salamander festival, and there might be a chance that some of the dogs would eat salamanders. Her suggestion that he "go bigger," expanding on the size of the dog park, within the 32 acres of Hance Park, would just be a small jump for him.

"Don't you want this to be bigger than big, Shades?" she asked. "If so, you can advertise directly to the dog owners in advance to come to your section of the park because, as you say, dog lovers are animal lovers; thus they will be salamander lovers."

"Yes, Laura," he said. "I think you nailed it."

# Chapter Eleven

At Madison Meadows Junior High School, Joe was overwhelmed and could not meet many of the challenges presented to him. It began to sink in how different he was, as nearly everyone at school managed to point it out, in one way or another. One of the cruelest times in life is when you know you are different from everyone else, especially when your classmates are eclipsing you in social status. Either you are on the inside, or you are on the outside looking in, and Joe definitely was on the outside.

Joe was smarter than all the other kids, as he, in his head, and on paper, had all the answers. It was the only thing he had going for him. In the halls, or during direct contact with other students, he had nothing. He was getting an F in his life at Madison Meadows, and there wasn't a tutor in the world that might raise that kind of grade.

During this difficult time, to say Joe was picked on was a huge understatement. He was relentlessly bullied. At first it was only the boys, as he was still thought of as cute enough for the girls to be curious about, but soon after, as things played out, he was fielding harassment from both sexes.

He was first noticed for his inability to use complete language, so he was often bombarded by questions from groups of mean kids, who would laugh at Joe's singular response. The questions came at him so fast, that he didn't have time to ignite the flying sound he needed to block them out. Some of the rapid fire questions were extremely inappropriate.

"Are you a Martian?"

"Yes."

"Do you beat off ten times a day?"

"Yes."

"Did you take LSD this morning?"

"Yes."

"Did Principal Collins have butt sex with you on the weekend?"

"Yes."

Each school day there were new questions, which seemed more and more hilarious to his classmates. He couldn't go from class to class without fielding these, on the fly, in the hallway.

Then there was gym class. Not only was Joe uninterested in sports, he was required to wear a uniform of school shorts and a gym shirt, which lumped out in places where his reduced cape had been pushed underneath. Even if Joe had been willing to explain the logical reason behind it all, it still would have been viewed as different and as strange.

All of these events broke Grace O'Halloran's heart. She accepted Joe as different, and the conversation she had with Joe's mother, at sixth grade graduation, reinforced her empathy toward him. Grace hated the bullies but didn't want to sacrifice her own social standing by sticking up for Joe when they rode him. She tried some other little things, such as sliding up to him at his locker and, at a volume no louder than a whisper, asking how he was doing. When he didn't answer, she encouraged him to hang in there. Joe anticipated these interactions, because this one act from Grace, he felt, was an example of the way people should be, and how they should treat him. He also began to anticipate other things he liked about her presence, such as how she smelled, the amount of curl in her hair, and what clothes she was wearing. Joe started to feel pleasurable physical reactions when she was near, and he wanted to stay close to her, but he also, at the same time, wanted to explode into flight, run down the hall, over and through anyone who was in his way. Joe was smart enough to know that all of this would potentially increase him being bullied.

Grace's heart during the first few months of junior high school wasn't the only one that broke. Joe's heart became broken too. Without Joe being consulted, Grace started going out with one of the most popular kids at Madison Meadows. She was always on the arm of a kid named Christopher, a star athlete, and one of the abusers in the group. When this happened, his own and Grace's interactions became less and less frequent. Joe felt he was more alone than ever, and all he had was himself to avoid the landmine of bullies he would face each day. Grace's boyfriend, at least, had stopped being a part of the bullying group, which Joe viewed as one less kid to ruin his day.

Right before winter vacation, and in the middle of one of the more searing hallway interrogations, Joe started anxiously flapping his arms. He was still saying 'yes,' to all questions, but he was failing greatly in his attempt to block out his anxiety. The group began to poke and push him, and Joe flapped harder and faster.

Suddenly, one of Joe's flaps connected with a loud slap to the side of one of the bully's heads, and the hallway suddenly became completely silent. It was as if someone had hit a reset button, and the lack of sound felt not only like the group had been placed on mute, but also like the entire world was quiet and weightless, and holding its breath.

\* \* \*

Afterward, Joe had to reconstruct the sequence of events in a linear manner, starting with the slap. Then there was the deafening silence after, completely contrasting the sharp sound of the slap, which seemed as loud as gunfire. In those few seconds of dead silence, Joe was at peace, but only in those few seconds, the ones before Grace screamed and Joe's consciousness blacked out. Was the slap he connected with so terrible that it caused someone else to scream? He heard the word which was screamed. It was the word, "stop." While reconstructing his memory of the incident, he thought the hallway seemed foggy, and combined with the brutal quiet, the entire scene no longer seemed of this world. He saw the faces of the mob. They were no longer laughing, or taunting; they were frozen from the moment of the slap. Joe surveyed the group. He saw no one bleeding. Why was there a scream? It was eerie. Joe wanted to scream. He may have. He wasn't sure. He felt completely outside his body during this time.

His hand hurt, and if his hand hurt, he must have hit someone, and was that someone the girl that was screaming? "No," he concluded. The scream was too far up the hall. It was not coming from the boy who was a few feet in front of him with the left side of his face red. He was the closest person. That person had been slapped.

And now that boy was lurching, almost hopping toward him, rearing back his fist, the way a pitcher threw a baseball. Joe wanted to duck. Something bad and painful was about to happen. He had seen

people punched in movies. The sound of the crowd was now mud-
dled, the volume building up to a loud rumble: the roar of a monster.
It was like no sound he had heard before. Joe wondered why, in general, sound distorted, and what was the relationship between that,
and him about to be hit.

Then there was a blur, just when Joe had started to flinch. It was
a big and large blur. *Was it the boy's fist, moving toward him, that had
distorted his vision?* All of the sensory items appeared to Joe like the
blur of speed he had witnessed, similar to the blur of George Reeves'
flight in the black-and-white *Adventures of Superman.* He was still
flinching, preparing for the punch, but now he sensed there was a
clear distortion of time. He knew he should have been hit already.
*Being hit should only take a split-second, shouldn't it?* He heard the
crowd's roar clearly now. *Had he been hit, and just not felt it, or even
noticed? Had he blacked it all out so that he couldn't feel the pain?*

Later, Joe knew it was not the case. His aggressor was thrown past
his right side, the body of it launched and made contact with Joe's
right shoulder, causing Joe to twist a little to his left. Then, Joe saw
what he didn't expect. There was someone tackling the boy who had
tried to punch him, from behind. That person had his attacker down
on the ground, shoulder digging deep into the bully's back, pinning
him. The girl who was the voice of the original scream was now right
in front of him. She was still screaming, but she was repeating to
him, "Joe. Are you alright? Are you alright?"

The crowd all started to repeat, 'yes,' over and over to any of her
questions, as Principal Collins, and a few other teachers arrived at the
scene. One of them pulled Grace's boyfriend off the other boy, and it
was then that Joe recognized Grace O'Halloran as the girl in front of
him asking the questions that the crowd was responding to. The two
boys were taken away by their arms, but not before Grace's boyfriend
turned to Joe, and said, "Hi, I'm Grace's boyfriend, Christopher. I
want you to know that Grace and I have your back. This shit is going
to end." His saying this changed something in the social pecking
order. Even though Joe was still on the outside, he was armed with
a new status. With this status, Joe had amnesty against harassment
for the rest of junior high.

# Chapter Twelve

After things had calmed down following Joe's incident at school, and Adrian was off from traveling, Millie flew to Cambridge for two weeks, to see her parents. She needed some time in the city she'd grown up in, so that she could feel, and remember, the person she used to be, and determine if she'd been better or worse than the person she was now. She wanted to use her time with her parents as a barometer to measure this, but this wasn't as cut-and-dry as she thought. Mostly, it was because she had to endure her parents, Richard and Samantha, who had hours of banal things to talk about with her. Their main topic was the changes in Harvard Square, and they gladly spoke of the pros and cons of each one, mostly the cons. In general, they liked the changes which got rid of the shabby businesses, as long as those changes didn't take away from the character of the square. They debated the colonial Gulf station's removal, as Samantha enjoyed the faux chicness of the white columns and the blue cupola, which were being replaced by The Inn at Harvard Square. Richard liked that a basically unneeded gas station was now an inn, a place which people concluded was "good for the economy."

Millie wondered if her parents' relationship had always been like this, and she'd just *felt* it was normal. She tried to focus on whether or not there were deeper feelings in their abundance of conversation; but as their conversations continued on the same path, day after day, she realized that there weren't. What Millie heard was that they both hated the Eliot Street Parking Garage, which shouldn't have been necessary anyway, with the new Red Line branching out to Alewife Station.

"At least it has real brick siding," Samantha added. "The gray cement parking garages they have in Boston are so darn ugly." Nearby,

the old Ha'Penny Pub and The Blue Parrot had been replaced by a
large brick and glass office building, One Mifflin Place. Her parents
liked the bricks, but even the bricks couldn't change their negative
opinions regarding the trends within Harvard Square.

"This is only the beginning of more yuppies, fewer locals," Richard
predicted. "Soon, there will be no Wursthaus, or Tasty. Just wait and
see. There will be a Burger King, and an IHOP in there."

"There will never be an IHOP in Harvard Square. Never. International?" Samantha added, "My tuches!"

"Oy vey," Richard responded, poking fun at his wife's goy appro-
priation of a Yiddish word. "We apparently are all international."

"How about we take a walk and check it out?" Samantha suggested to Millie. "You may not even recognize the place."

Millie wrestled with the idea. On one hand she always loved the
ten or so minute walk to Harvard Square, but on the other, a twenty-
five degree day in January, considered a warm day in the middle of
winter for her parents, would be torturous to her after living over a
decade in Phoenix. Plus, her parents would want to stop and point
things out, while the wind was blowing through the oversized coat
she'd had to borrow from her mother.

"At some point maybe," Millie fibbed, knowing that if she were
to go on that walk, she would have to make many stops inside the
warmer ports of retail stores in order to warm up.

"So Adrian didn't want to come?" Samantha asked. It was the
third or fourth time since Millie's plane touched down she'd been
asked this question, after being asked multiple times about it via telephone, before she left.

"Mom, he has to work, and also, take care of Joe."

"Joe needs to learn to take care of himself. He's almost a teenager."

"I'm working on it," Millie said.

"Well, the last time we were there, he seemed all wrapped up in
things that didn't matter," Richard cut in. "Maybe we need to visit
more often. Give him some more input."

"I really thought you'd be there more often," she replied.

"We're not as young as we used to be," Samantha said.

The last time the Englanders visited had been six months ago, after
Joe's elementary school graduation. The Gamuts' life at home seemed
to Millie and Adrian to be on track, but it seemed to be off the track
for the Englanders. The Englanders noticed all the things an outsider

looking in would. It made them not want to visit at all, being that Joe was the way he was. And, he had been assaultive to Samantha years earlier. In the back of her mind, Millie knew that her mother was so anti-violent that she would never understand Joe's slap, or his challenges, and that she certainly did not wish to spend much time with him.

"R, it's like they live in a purple house, and all the other houses on the block are white," Samantha had said, at the time, "and they are so used to it, that it doesn't seem purple anymore."

Millie and Adrian felt otherwise. They both knew the house was metaphorically purple. Millie accepted the purple house for what it was, a different colored house in a dull, white-painted-house neighborhood. It wasn't the worst thing in the world. Adrian's take was to just stay out of the neighborhood, both literally and figuratively, try to ignore the differences in colors, and hope maybe they would go away. When the Englanders came to Arizona, they flew all these doubts front and center in Adrian's head.

Here, in Cambridge, in their white home with black shutters, as in every other house between Harvard Square and Fresh Pond Parkway, the Englanders felt safe, both literally and figuratively. They continued to tag-team their daughter regarding her solo visit, even though they had no plans themselves on coming back to Arizona and seeing Adrian and Joe. Under their interrogation, it didn't take too long for Millie to confess that things weren't going too well between her and Adrian, and she needed a break from there to think about what she wanted to do.

"Think about it? Are you thinking about getting a divorce?" Samantha asked.

"Well, if that's what she wants...," Richard answered.

"... and divorce is so common these days, R," Samantha finished. "It's the norm."

"Exactly, S! Millie could get a job around here, and the schools in Cambridge would be perfect for Joe!"

"Hold it right there!" Millie interrupted, with a bold flourish. "I've not said anything about leaving Adrian, moving back to live here, or anything of the sort. I just need some time to get away for a few weeks, and feel like myself again. I was feeling virtually trapped in my house, and I thought this was a good idea. Good God!"

"Well, you don't have to use such profane language," Samantha added.

"Yes, good God, Millie, please! You know how S does not like that." Richard said, without irony, although both her parents knew their daughter's defiance, and what it meant. They knew Millie had considered all of her options, even divorce, and was now steadfast, and being adamant about her decision to stay in her marriage. It was her choice she was going to defend to the death. But what they didn't know was that Millie, based on her time in Cambridge, was fortifying her communication with Adrian, committing to a goal that the two of them would never chatter just to take up time, never use superficial conversation to fill the empty spaces in their lives.

# Chapter Thirteen

Joe missed his mother, as it was just he and his dad at home. It was a pretty basic situation. Mom was away visiting his grandparents. He wanted to be there too, but not because of the grandparents, as he'd avoided them completely during their last visit to Arizona; after all, there were "a lot of things going on after graduation." When his mother called, she told him it was cold and snowy in Cambridge, and she had to dress warmly. The thought of bundling up in a heavy coat, a pair of gloves, a hat, and a scarf, gave Joe mixed signals. The snug coat would feel good, tight and safe, like a scarf around his head; but a scratchy, not quite right hat, would challenge Joe to keep it together.

Joe also felt that spending time with his father was like being on a long line in the supermarket or pharmacy. Joe hated those situations, in which he just wanted to scream but knew that screaming wouldn't make the line move any quicker. His father was trying. Joe thought his attempts during these fourteen days to get Joe to speak and to do things with him were worth noting, even if the interactions made his skin crawl the way a rough piece of fabric felt when it rubbed against his bare epidermis.

His mother was good at knowing when things were about to get overwhelming to him. Without her, Joe worried how his father would anticipate what might happen. Joe knew his father wanted to protect him from anything bad, but he was more of a Clark Kent than a Superman type. To compensate, for these fourteen days, Laura took Joe out more. Laura was kind and had good instincts about giving him space when needed. Still, Laura, for all her good—and just like his father—never could quite recognize, with one-hundred percent accuracy, when situations were about to become critical. Even being around her sometimes, in itself, would be stimulus producing. On the days Laura wore the kind of clothes Steven disapproved of, Joe felt the same stirring as he had when Grace spoke softly into his ear near his locker, her soft hair tickling his ear. It wasn't as if Laura's clothes were scandalous one bit, but Joe was nearing his prime, and the involuntary hormonal rush, which came with him becoming a teenaged boy, was potent. Laura had noticed and treated it as the normal, natural occurrence it was. Why not? She was an attractive woman in her early thirties, and of course, men and boys had been like bees to honey around her ever since she was Joe's age. The fact that she wore a Catholic cross around her neck also increased the curiosity around her.

In a way, Laura was relieved about Joe's reaction. It seemed more normal than abnormal to her, as she had vast experience in dealing with men with hard-ons around her. That was the normal. It pleased her that this reaction was something which made Joe just like everybody else, instead of being totally different.

Laura ignored the involuntary action happening in Joe's pants, and kept taking him to Barney's Costumes. These trips served dual purposes in this regard. First, she wanted Joe to form a bond with Shades Creek, the Salamander Festival proprietor, over their love of salamanders. Interacting with Shades would eliminate his focus on her. Second, the majesty of the amazing Superman outfit, trumped any sort of attention on her or anything else.

What Laura did not know was that Joe found salamanders more interesting in books than scurrying around in glass tanks. Focusing on them with their quick movements tended to overstimulate him. At Barney's, the blue suit and red cape was the perfect thing to focus on, so he never paid attention to anything else, nor had he ever even learned Shades' name. Joe just assumed that his name was Barney.

When they returned home, it was more time with his dad, walking on egg shells, and trying not to get outside of himself, keeping things simple, and without conflict. Joe wished that he understood why he had his minor blackouts during extreme times of stress and anxiety. The blackouts usually began with a stressful event, his heart racing so fast that he could hear the accelerated heartbeat loudly in his head. The sound became louder and louder, until it was almost the only thing he heard. Shifted way into the background were the real senses, now processed as distorted sound, distorted light, and distorted vision. He felt he was trapped outside of reality, and he would try to stop it by flapping and moving his arms. Then, often, when he came out of it, it was to the sights and sounds of the aftermath—one where he may have hurt someone, or something had been broken—followed by the shame of it all: the terrible shame of who he was and what he had done, and the knowledge that it was all utterly beyond his control.

When Joe was younger, his 'yessing' kept things safe, but now simply agreeing could induce conflict, as it prevented him from doing what *he* wanted to do. All he wanted to do was sit in his room, watch movies, listen to the radio, and read books about reptiles and nature. It was a good way to avoid things. Even simple requests, such as setting the table for dinner, caused him a great deal of anxiety. When Joe felt this coming on, he reached for the towel around his neck and became a superhero. He flew around the house, chased away evil in the world, and ignored any real demands that were made or that might be placed on him. He flew faster and faster, until again, fragile objects broke in his wake. At times he wanted to ditch the cape, feeling that it pointed out his differences to his classmates, but as much as he might have wanted, he couldn't let go of it. It was a way to focus inward, and by doing that, he was able to overcome his severe anthropophobic reaction, his now severe generalized fear of nearly all people or situations except for the ones involving Laura or his mother. Even his Superman flying noise had begun to change how it looked and sounded. It had morphed into a quick inhale and exhale sound, akin to hyperventilation. His cheeks would puff in and out quickly, which indicated, only to those close to him, that he was close to, or already in, a panic, which was now quite serious. Often his panics took him to near or complete blackout, and to other levels of dissociation.

The pre-winter hallway episode succeeded in eliminating further bullying. At least now at school he felt like a quiet outsider, even though people knew who he was. In his mind, he had blended into the crowd, but, in reality, Joe was a known person, endorsed by a popular couple, whose endorsement was now supported by the entire football and winter track team. He also was supported by nearly the full class of girls, who wished to be as popular, and on the same high social level, as Grace. Joe now had an escort in the hallway, protecting him if anything were to happen. It was almost as if he were a mascot, a beloved person in a costume who didn't have to speak to anyone. The jocks, and the popular want-to-be social climbers, had his back, and they always seemed to be in his vicinity. It felt to Joe that he was a car that was being followed on city streets, or on a highway, which he only noticed when he focused on them; and unlike some of the tails in the Superman shows and movies, they were good. He didn't need to shake them.

# Chapter Fourteen

Adrian figured he had been given two weeks to bond with his son, and this was his goal. He calculated that if he completed exactly three bonding actions every day, his and Joe's relationship would improve. On day one, he wore the blue suit and tie, watched a Superman movie, and attempted to read a book with him in his room. Joe, who always read alone, pulled the book from Adrian's hands, and moved to sit on his bed with it. Adrian didn't anticipate why Joe had answered, 'yes,' to him asking if he wanted to be read to, when he could have just gone on his bed by himself to begin with. Afterward, he figured that maybe Joe felt he was too old to be read to. Adrian thought, *if only he could really fly*. That would certainly make an impression.

Adrian knew that you got back results from whatever you put into something. He also knew that for every reaction, there is an equal and opposite reaction. It was a measurable equation, like when you plug a number into a spreadsheet and the result pops out as a different number which had been affected. Adrian felt with Joe, it seemed that things always remained basically the same no matter what he did; his son didn't want to talk to him, and he barely interacted with him. He certainly was trying to the best of his ability, but when he felt frustrated by the lack of results, it showed, which caused Joe to withdraw even further, to seek solitude in his room. All of this flabbergasted Adrian, as how could a kid who ... who looked to be quite typical, act in such non-normal ways? It didn't follow the equation which you could input into most kids, and generate a desired result.

Joe perked up on the weekend when Laura came by. It was a nice break for Adrian too, even though he had worked all week, and Joe had been at school. Adrian's head felt fatigued and dull, as it might feel if he had gently banged it against a wall. Contrasting all that was Laura, in her light summer clothes, gold cross around her neck, looking somewhat like the wholesome young woman you might find in a chewing gum commercial. Now in her thirties, Laura still got carded when she bought beer, and often received suspicious looks when they read the birthdate on her license. In fact, she seemed to attract looks wherever she went. Adrian made sure he never looked at her in any way that would be interpreted as libidinous, because that would cause an unintentional result, one he would never, ever, want to happen. Adrian was never that type of a person anyways. He knew the sanctity of marriage was also a contract. The only woman he would ever consider making love to for the rest of his life would be Millie, and it would be done in a tried and true way, which usually was satisfactory for each of them.

He did happen to notice Joe looking at her in a funny way, but it was something which didn't modify Laura's behavior. He wondered if possibly Joe had developed a little crush on her. After all, she was always describing him as a handsome boy, which he was, but it was always said in a way that most people would not find flirtatious. He hoped that Joe wouldn't act out in any way which might ruin things or make others feel uncomfortable, as the prospect of not having Laura's support, not just with Joe, but with Millie, would be dire. Adrian made sure that he observed both Laura and Joe when they returned home for any signs of dysfunction. He found that when they returned from their exploits, things seemed exactly the same as they were when they'd left, and thank God for that.

\* \* \*

When Millie returned home, things about her didn't seem much different to Adrian either. In Adrian's sweetest day dream, she would return home, with him and Joe sitting at the dinner table discussing their days. This was not the case. Instead, when Millie arrived, Joe was in his room listening to music while reading, and Adrian was in the living room, watching *Law and Order*. Millie was sweaty from still wearing the heavy winter clothes from Massachusetts. She stood in front of him, kissed his cheek, and told him she missed him and that they should talk more with each other. Then she entered Joe's room, and Adrian wondered if he suddenly was hearing things, or if it was just the sound of his television program. He turned down the volume, and heard two distinct voices, one being Millie's and the other, much lower, definitely not the voice of the disc-jockey from Joe's radio. Adrian approached the partially closed door and heard, "I missed you." Quickly he pushed upon the door, but all the sound and motion of the room stopped.

"Joe, I heard you talk!" Adrian said excitedly, which caused Joe to step back, as Adrian's voice, in loud decibels, bounced harshly off the four walls. "Did you just say something to your mother?"

"Yes."

"I heard it. Joe, I heard it!"

"Yes."

"I want you to know that you can speak anytime in front of me," Adrian added, noting immediately he hadn't said, 'to me,' but rather a more distant term, 'in front of me.'

"Yes."

Millie noted that this mode of questioning could go on for a long time, which would only serve to agitate both Joe and Adrian. She turned to Adrian and was flat and direct, "He wasn't talking to you."

All three of them stopped. Millie's statement was true, logical, and sad for Adrian. He was used to Millie's strength in identifying the crux of all social interactions, in ways he never could; so he trusted everything she said to be fact in this regard, and in Adrian's world, facts were never questioned.

"I'm sorry," he said to both Millie and Joe. "I won't do that again." Adrian's words also were absolute truths, and truths were something he always held on to. After this interaction with his wife and son, Adrian never questioned or forced Joe's speech, and he never again tried to overhear him behind a closed door. He accepted the fact that Joe could speak, though not to anyone but Millie. He accepted that Joe was smart, and that was a reality he'd known for years, and reality was also things which didn't need to be questioned. Adrian, for the rest of his life, would never hear, or again, overhear, his son saying another word besides 'yes,' because now it made sense.

# Chapter Fifteen

While Joe had encompassing filters, Laura had the polar opposite, hardly any at all. She let Millie know how much she missed her while she was away, and she let Steven know how confined she felt in her marriage. Like her friend, she felt trapped, and especially when Millie was away, Laura's life consisted of work, home, sleep, seeing Joe, and managing her crew of unique personalities. It was the strange ones who were the most interesting, even when treated or medicated, as they all had such an interesting take and energy on things. Her husband had the worst kind of energy. He was the person with the biggest problems, who swore he didn't have any problems. Laura would cringe at the thought of their next interaction. Since she no longer wanted to feel controlled, she took the role of calling Steven on his bullshit, and accepting the consequences of his anger. At least it was something which he had no say on.

Millie was her rock. She was a woman who, when dealt a bad hand, played it, and played it well. Did she have challenges with Joe? Certainly, she did. Did she have the greatest marriage in the world? Certainly, she did not. Yet, in both examples, she remained positive, and instead of wallowing, she redirected her energy toward helping others who had struggles. It was how Millie managed her challenges. Her perseverance, her outlook, and her ability to come out in the best place possible, were traits Laura envied. Millie, herself, recognized these strong traits, and they were the traits, she told Laura, she wanted to give back to the world.

Laura started inviting Millie over to The Good Sam for lunch when she was on break. She wished there was time to go to a real restaurant, and not sit in her nurse's uniform in the cafeteria, a setting which she felt represented the hospital's class system. In this system, the patients ate in their locked wards while somber-looking family members huddled in support at tables where they ate comfort foods: grilled cheese, BLTs, tomato soup or chili. The nurses sat with other nurses, and the doctors all sat together, not acknowledging any of the others outside their castes. Their conversations, usually work related, danced around the borders of confidentiality, unless they spoke about their cases in code, which created a new layer of exclusiveness. Laura liked to take her lunch outside, even if the scorching temperature painted the thermometer a bold red. She would remind herself, *"When I'm on break, it is important to use it as a break. Otherwise there would be no rest for me in my work state, and then what's the point of taking a break, if it's not a break?"* She said this as a mantra, each time she grabbed a sandwich and walked briskly past co-workers offering an open seat for her to join them.

She further defied all the unwritten hospital lunch rules by inviting an outsider to join her and chat about life. She even cheated an extra seven minutes on these days, the perfect number not to round up to the next quarter hour on her time card. She was excited about her time with Millie, but, because of their conversations, there would be the challenge to finish anything she ordered in time. Today she went with a bowl of already prepared gazpacho. Millie's salad looked slick and on its last gasps before becoming compost.

"Certainly not as fresh as Souper Salad's," Laura noted, halfway through the lunch break. The salad's freshness didn't seem to bother Millie as she picked at it—it not mattering whether she ate it or not, because honestly, she wasn't there for the lunch. Millie was there for Laura, to support her and suggest options in her life—options which Laura herself might not be able to foresee playing out in her life.

"You know, I've looked into leaving Adrian," Millie said.

"No! Really?" Laura stammered. "I mean, you told me some things, but I didn't think you would have taken it that far!"

"Well, after visiting my parents, I decided I'm not going to. It was just good to go away. You should consider it."

Laura had considered it; in fact, she had longed for a break from Steven, every single day. "I don't think I can. I'm really busy at work... and besides," she hesitated, "I don't think Steven would be too happy."

"Maybe you need a break. I think you could use one," Millie said.

Laura thought of her mental state and how it would feel to go home and sit in the sun any time she wanted, like she did during her lunch breaks. She so needed breaks from Steven, and if she wasn't allowed to take them in the ways she wanted, even the small daily ones, what was the use of taking a break? She ached to have small breaks from the insanity of him. Then it struck her. *What if I take a much longer break?*

# Chapter Sixteen

Joe concluded that it only took a few people initially to be on some-one's side in order for many to find it acceptable to join them. Those extra supporters were like him, on the outskirts, looking for an in, and once the ice had been broken, they could be on the side of someone with obvious differences. That conclusion brought Joe hope, as all he had to do was convince one person, *one person*, that he was okay, that he was functional and he was smart. He certainly didn't want to stand out, especially standing out as someone weird. He knew he looked good enough not to be confused by sight as someone with de-velopmental issues. The only thing which people would be confused about would be his communication problem, mistaken for his being shy.

The people he had to sell himself to were the ones who had in-fluence, who spoke up on his behalf. Growing up, it was his mother. Mothers are great fighters, great advocates, or at least, they should be. Millie was strong in her opinions and her values, which helped Joe considerably. Next there was Laura, who also never saw him in a bad light.

At school, support started with Grace and advanced with Christo-pher, which saved his life there. In a way, Joe was lucky that he didn't have to be dragged into the normal social dynamics of the world, the many people to please, and the popularity ladder, where the drama was often devastating. He had these four people, with their outer circle of underlings, and that was enough for Joe Gamut.

Joe wasn't quite as sure about his father or his grandparents within this model. They seemed to be part of the underlings, but they should really be more a part of the solution. Joe felt he appreciated them, but the love he wanted to feel seemed empty. He knew they tried hard, but all of it should have been more instinctual, or natural, and it wasn't. Adrian and the Englanders had to put forth an effort, and Joe wished they didn't, that things would just come to them. For this reason, he didn't feel completely accepted and safe around them. The people that anticipated things before they happened were much safer than the *wait and see what happens* people. If there was a choice between hanging out with those people and going into his room to read books and listen to music, he'd choose to be alone in his room.

This had other advantages as well. Joe had a love of the written word, not just because books presented facts which he absorbed like a sponge, but because he saw writing, instead of speaking, as a way for him to be direct and concise, proving his worth in the world. He didn't use writing for personal communication, such as responses to questions, as why would he get out of his non-conflictual 'yes,' mode, using writing as a means to create conflict? He did produce notes to people if he needed help during some of his independence trainings in the community, as long as there was no chance of a negative encounter. Earlier that week he'd passed a note to a stock-boy at Albertsons Supermarket which requested the location of shoe laces. Information gathering, Joe concluded, was a totally appropriate and safe use of writing.

Joe also excelled in writing at school. The academic use of writing gave Joe the opportunity to prove to others he wasn't stupid; in fact, it proved that he was one of the smartest pupils in his Madison Meadows Junior High School class. Any assignment graded for oral or class participation, Joe was allowed accommodation for, so his grades were always A's.

In his room, music provided a different experience. Joe felt that songs were telling him things as well, the same way he learned lessons with Superman. Because of Superman, he believed people could prevent and fight bad things, or get places, and then leave places in a blink of an eye. He knew that literally people didn't fly, but mentally and figuratively, he fully bought into it. Kids at school figuratively *flew* all the time, and he saw it each time a classmate avoided a conflict without freezing up. The hope was that given his makeup, he could learn these skills to save himself. This started with just a sound, the flying sound he made, but the more he thought about it, the further his idea of safety in flying, by making sounds, needed to advance.

The songs though represented a different hope. Joe saw that singing was a method people used to communicate without having to talk. He envisioned all of the singers not having any communication skills, and the singing was a way to announce love, angst, heartbreak, wants, and desires. Joe knew that he would never sing, the same way he could never fly, but there was again a hope that there were different ways to do things, and all Joe had to do was find his own way—without singing, without taking flight, to make it happen. Other people were doing things like singing and flying all the time; even if they weren't literally singing and flying, they communicated.

His mother had different ideas about Joe's ability to advance in life. Joe understood the reason why she was pushing. His mother was pushing to get him out of his shell, to get him to do the things other people did. Joe had just recently become a teenager, but his mother needed to teach him skills normal for someone twice his age. Those skills would be important down the road, because she mentioned it all the time, using a phrase which made the hair on Joe's arms feel like paper cuts.

"Joe," she would say, "you can't depend on us forever, as we won't be here for that long." Joe couldn't fly, and Joe couldn't sing, but somehow handling a budget and shopping for food were ways in which he could succeed in life without them. These were the silent non-super lifesavers which he knew would save him, with no singing or flying required.

# Chapter Seventeen

Millie's trip to Massachusetts was a nice respite, and she came back energized and refreshed. She looked at Adrian's positive traits the way she used to, and knew what she had to work on for Joe to be out on his own some day. She also felt able to do things out of the house now, while the men could have time with each other. She now considered working, or advancing her degree, because the burden of her responsibility to be the emotional rock in the household seemed to have been diminished, in a good way. Millie felt renewed, and for the first time since she had birthed Joe, she was ready to really begin her own life. As a strong, independent woman, she was convinced of that, and it seemed really odd, in retrospect, that she hadn't considered having her own career.

It wasn't financial reasons that held her back. There was always enough money, but that wasn't the reason she never worked. The fact was that Adrian made so much money at his job they never had to balance their checkbook. In the back of her mind, she suddenly felt she needed a back-up plan. Was Adrian always going to be there? Earning her degree would be a good Plan B, but above that, Millie wanted to live her life on her terms, and not just to be there to process and figure out the world for the rest of her family.

It took Adrian no time to process what Millie wanted. He was 100% supportive, and encouraged whatever would make her happy. Millie wished his support were more emotional, rather than filling in the variables he knew of a "happy marriage equation," but nevertheless, she was grateful. She was also grateful that Adrian seemed to be responding to her push for deeper communication with her, even if it started slowly. Considering that just a few weeks ago they were on the, "How was your day?" level, Millie was encouraged that Adrian might just be able to evolve in more ways than she had been willing to believe.

Upon returning, she also wanted to see Laura more. Laura continued to see Joe weekly, but Millie wanted her own Laura-time, so she was thrilled when they started meeting at The Good Sam for lunch. She wanted Laura's advice about attending school, and the best way to upgrade her psychology credentials. She knew a Master's Degree would help further her career the way she desired, and graduate school could be worked on part-time. Then, after Joe was in college, she could have full days to finish her degree, and she could begin in the workplace about the time he graduated. Millie also felt that her decision to stick it out, and improve her less-than-perfect marriage, empowered her into a role of helping Laura move away from her terrible marriage, a union Laura said was never going to be viewed as more perfect, or even equal.

If Millie noticed Laura seemed sadder, it seemed that Joe was just the opposite. In private, he no longer said that he didn't want to go to school in the morning. He hinted at having friends or having people watching out for him. Maybe the independence trainings she worked on with him had generalized into some new social component. It was hard to tell because Joe's private times were his, and Millie entering into her teenager's world had become more and more difficult.

After leaving Cambridge, Millie was confident she understood three of the most important people in her life, two of whom she always felt would understand her forever. Millie knew that moving in this direction brought her more self-alliance, which led to greater contentment.

# Chapter Eighteen

As junior high flew by with Joe staying in good standing, the inevitable *what's next* waited in front of him like a blank canvas, but Joe felt he didn't have any paint or brushes. Joe liked schedules, and predictability, and didn't like open and random thoughts of the future. When Joe didn't feel safe, he would completely embrace familiar things—whether people, places, or things—which fit into expected situations or outcomes.

His mother drilled into him what he could expect, and what would be next in his life. This script, in itself, became a routine, or a scheduled event he shared with his mom. Per his mother's tutoring, Joe was able to successfully make a list of grocery items which were needed to sustain him for one week. He would pass them in to her on Thursday, making sure he was not duplicating previous lists, which he knew by rote, and which would be easy to produce automatically. To make his list he would first start with a grid where he would fill in seven breakfasts, seven lunches, and seven dinners. Then he would transpose the grid onto his final list; for example, seven breakfasts meant three boxes of Raisin Bran, and one gallon of Lucerne 2% reduced-fat milk. Seven lunches meant a loaf of bread, three-quarters of a pound of lunch meat, five-eighths of a pound of cheese, a sleeve of cookies, and a small bag of apples. Specific lunch items, such as which meat or cookies he would buy, would be selected based on what was on sale. Joe would then complete his list with what he would call his wild card items, on a separate row. These included chips, butterscotch hard candies, and perhaps a box of the cracker, *de la semaine*, his clever word play on *du jour*. Joe developed a great deal of pride about his lists.

Joe found that what really screwed things up in his head, was when his father was home and started eating *his* items, especially the tasty wild cards. He would, of course, ask Joe if he could eat them, and Joe would, of course, say, 'yes,' but Joe would inevitably head to his room angry and not wanting any disagreement. His mother would settle him down saying, it was only a list of items which was important for when he lived alone, and outsider interference such as this would not exist during that time. Then Joe would hear his mother scold his father about the food and taking advantage of Joe's penchant to agree with everything. This made Joe feel safe, but when the time came for Joe to shop at Albertsons without her or Laura's help, he had a lot of questions.

"All you have to do is bring the list," his mother told him. "You don't have to talk to anyone."

"What happens if they don't have what's on the list?" he said.

"Oh, that market is really big. I don't think that will be a problem," his mother reassured him. "Albertsons is a big store."

On Saturday, his mother pulled into Albertsons lot, but Joe wouldn't leave the car, so she drove him home. The following Saturday, Joe entered the store, but returned to the car without any items. This was progress. The following Saturday, it was one step further, as his mother stood at Albertsons door, while Joe filled the shopping cart. She was the one that took the cart to checkout. It was a big comfort to know she was there, even if she was not flanking him. The next week, he shopped, and both of them went up to the register.

By the end of two months, the plan was for his mother to stand by the door half the time, and then, at a point when Joe was out of sight, she would return to the car. On this day, it all started out well. Joe was smoothly heading down the aisles, picking out what he needed. Then, something he had not expected happened. Albertsons was out of gallons of Lucerne 2% reduced-fat milk. They had gallons of 1% low-fat, and of whole milk, and even half-gallons of the 2%, but Joe was frozen in front of the refrigerated section. What should he pick that wouldn't be wrong? Would his mother be mad if he failed?

Joe started to touch each of the options, and selected a gallon of the 1% low-fat—his best-laid back-up plan. Still, with milk in hand, he was frozen in front of the dairy section. A small log jam began to form—by other customers who wanted to buy milk. Their carts clanged against Joe's, and people bristled by, or reached over, or around, the space occupied by Joe. He started making the flying noise, as he needed to get out of there. He wanted to, but the gaggle of people surrounding him was spiking his anxiety, and he was stuck stationary.

"Excuse me," one said.

"Yes."

"Could you move?"

"Yes."

"Get out of my way, please."

"Yes."

"Move!" said a third, as each customer seemed to be more and more impatient with him.

Suddenly, and without any self-regulation, Joe spiked the plastic milk bottle on the floor, and created an upward wave of milk, which splashed on Joe and two of the customers. Joe, now in complete Superman panic mode, began to fly through the aisles with his cart. He bulldozed over another shopping cart, flattened a cardboard vitamin display, and banged hard against the store's automatic exit door, which opened too slow to let him out as quickly as he needed to leave.

\* \* \*

Millie knew something had happened, as Joe's uncontrolled sprint toward her with a full shopping cart had left a dent in her new Saturn sedan; he had struck it harder than even the dent resistant side-panels could resist. As she got out of the car, she noticed two men, a security guard, and the Albertsons' manager, sprinting and shouting across the shimmer of the heat-distorted parking lot, and headed their way. The security guard was young, perhaps a student at the university, and he advanced quickly, every stride winning a race against the Mr. Whipple-looking manager.

Millie thrust her body between the possible aggressors and her son, but she was nearly knocked over by the boy security officer who attempted to reach through her to grab Joe by the collar of his shirt. Joe jumped away, which left the boy yanking on to Joe's terrycloth cape, and left the choked Joe gasping for air. Millie now grabbed at the boy's wrists, attempting to dislodge him from her son, as Whipple became involved in a series of inane questions of the, *"Do you know you have to pay for these items?"* variety.

Millie tried to answer, quickly attempting to give Joe's history, while she continued to wrestle with the kid security officer, who was now red in the face, his sweaty lower arms continuing to slip out of Millie's grasp. The two continued to grapple, as the resistance increased around Joe's neck until Joe lost consciousness, and Millie had slugged the boy in the face.

\* \* \*

Ambulances bring police, and there were suddenly two vehicles in the parking lot at Albertsons. Joe was alright; his breathing came back on its own after less than fifteen seconds. Millie explained, this time more calmly, Joe's behavioral history to the police; but unfortunately, she had to do it at 16030 North 56th Street, the City of Phoenix Police Department, Desert Horizon Precinct, where she and Joe had been transferred. Security boy had been transferred there too, for his role in Joe's strangulation, and faced possible charges himself. As they were both being interviewed, Joe read the large yellow, red, and green, promotional poster over and over again, which listed the City of Phoenix Police Department, Desert Horizon Precinct, as one of the sponsors of Phoenix's first annual Salamander Festival.

# Chapter Nineteen

Thanks to its generous sponsors the first Salamander Festival in Phoenix was a resounding success. It was mostly because of the front page coverage in the *Arizona Republic, The Daily Star*, and the *East Valley Tribune*, as well as all the brightly-colored posters, hung all over the downtown area. The local television news even picked up the story. Two of the affiliates interviewed Shades Creek, while another prominently featured Laura Wellin, who spoke while Shades sat next to her. The television reporter even had the audacity to suggest flirtatiously that Laura become the first Salamander Queen; to this suggestion, Shades interrupted with, "This ain't about no queens. This is about the salamanders. They can become extinct, you know." It was just the beginning of the quirky Shades becoming a local celebrity.

So on the first Saturday in May, 1999, a decent crowd of around 5,000 showed up at Hance Park to partake in all the hoopla and celebration. Shades' booth, with his live salamanders, received a lot of attention, only because of Shades rather than the salamanders. He had thought his booth might be a big draw, being that the festival was about salamanders, but hadn't realized that people would be wanting to meet him. The children's events—face painting and the inaugural "Run Like a Salamander" race—did slightly better, but it was the food and drink stations which received the most attention. Many of the local restaurants creatively named their offerings with clever salamander names, which people loved. The Chicago Hamburger Company offered up a Mexican Salsa-Mander Burger, which was their usual cheeseburger with salsa, and Rips Bar offered up Salamander Shots to get "ripped" with. Almost all adults who got ripped, decided to paint their faces too, and some who were shirtless received full-torso paint. Shades didn't know how he felt about any of this, or how it related to species extinction, but he knew he was making a fair amount of money, enough to run the festival for the next few years and promote his love of the salamander.

Shades also thought that the promotional use of Barney's Costumes would help out that business for the rest of the year. He didn't have any salamander costumes in stock yet, so he wore a purple Barney the Dinosaur costume, which he normally kept hidden in the back of the shop, since he'd never wanted to associate his store with that awful children's musical program. Shades placed a placard around his neck, which stated his name as "Barneymander," a name not at all as clever as ones invented by the places like Rips or The Chicago Hamburger Company. The use of Barney, the purple dinosaur, was perhaps, in Shade's mind, the biggest failure of the festival, but he had a few years to do better in this department.

Laura was indeed named the Salamander Festival of Phoenix's first queen. Shades, after it was all said and done, had thought it was a good idea. The original television interviewer even tracked Laura down for a live interview, and then asked for another more private interview with her, after the festival was over.

"Oh, no thanks," she said politely to him, knowing that he was no longer being professional. "I think I'll vacate my throne immediately after today."

"But the interview really has nothing to do with you being the queen," the slick reporter said.

"Oh, I know that. Thanks for covering the festival," she said, not wanting any retaliation from this rejection to make its way onto the news in any way negative for the festival. It all reminded Laura that she had options in men any time she wanted; but being married, she would not ever act on them. Anytime she faced this reminder, it made her resent Steven for not appreciating exactly what he had.

Shades, even though the festival turned into more of a celebration of food and drink than of salamanders, was still happy for the financial success and the media coverage it received. He finished up the event with a heartfelt speech, thanking those who attended, and he vowed that this festival would be Phoenix's own, and something to be proud of. He concluded with the idea that it would be something the city was going to be known for. As delusional as it sounded, the crowd let out a loud cheer.

Joe was one who didn't let out a loud cheer, as Joe's 'yes' to want-

ing to go to the Salamander Festival with Laura had been vetoed by
Millie, who knew his 'yes,' was his typical disingenuous answer. It
was a fact Laura knew also, but Laura was still willing to take him
for his own social good, a push which Millie appreciated, although,
certainly after the recent police involvement, she was playing it safe.
It would have been a horrible environment for Joe to be in the middle of. Millie knew that at a crowded festival, as well as at any other
location, so many things could potentially go wrong.

# Part V

# Chapter One

Although Joe was being prepared for increased independence, he still wasn't able to successfully communicate the things he really wanted to do, versus the things he did not want to do or which would be a bad match for him. It angered him that he would freeze instead of giving a truthful response to questions, and that his 'yesses' caused an inner conflict while they were working functionally to stifle the outer conflict.

His bedroom was always a safe place. He had no conflict there. Books, music, and now, a new computer, passed the time. His Superman's cape and tee-shirt, although he still felt they were needed, seemed to not be as much in the forefront of his mind, because he knew the truth. The truth was that neither the costume nor the persona helped when it came to the key element of speaking or dealing with difficult situations. What it did was to provide a reminder that there was an out, though sometimes messy, when he needed to leave anything seemingly stressful. It didn't help while he was actually in those situations. For example, he did manage to get out of Albertsons, but he'd made a mess while he was in there, and it ended with police involvement. After that disaster, he told his mother he never wanted to go back to Albertsons. He chose not to fail there ever again; but as his mother vetoed his suggestion, she told him there would be better days and better times, doing what he had failed to do that day.

"Do you not go to a school with a lot of people in the halls, Joe? It's just a matter of getting used to what might happen," his mother said. His father thought therapy might be helpful, but Joe and his mother knew it would be an hour session of hundreds of 'yesses.'

Also to consider was there would be a new school next year, which started in August, and then, four years later, there would be college.

The biggest conflict Joe had, besides the kids in the hall being physically bigger, was that the sports teams of Sunnyslope High School were the Vikings, and as far as he knew, no Viking had ever conquered anything, or stepped foot anywhere close to Arizona. They might as well have been called the Sunnyslope Blizzards, as that name seemed to hold the same degree of truth and honesty. Then, there was the statue. Joe had noticed the silver and green colored Viking on their tour of Sunnyslope High, his green shield adorned with a giant 'S.' The ugly mascot, named Victor, was made of fiberglass, using a standard sea raider mold, with the same pose and measurements as the statue used by a well-known muffler company. Surrounding this atrocity was a brick wall, extended by an iron fence, so students wouldn't climb on Victor. The fence did very little to hold back the pile of drink boxes and food items that were tossed at Victor Viking daily. Joe worried if their Viking statue got barraged by the students, what would happen to the actual students, then ones less popular than a mascot? Would Joe still be revered, and protected at high school, the way he was in junior high? What happened if Grace and Christopher broke up? Would Christopher then move from a friend to, potentially, a foe? It was all these internal questions, which he could not defend against, that stayed circling inside Joe's head, and caused a constant drip of fresh anxiety, analogous to Chinese water torture.

# Chapter Two

Adrian had worked at AON six months shy of fifteen years. He could retire comfortably in another ten, but he couldn't see himself doing that. He absolutely loved his job, and if he could, he would work there until he died.

AON had already begun to prepare for the Y2K meltdown of their data system. It was rumored that all data would either be lost, become visible to others, or be corrupted in some way. The aspect of this unknown worried him, because—if those were the choices, were they the only ones possible? AON had not, as it seemed, narrowed down any of the good possibilities. But Millie had told him that whatever was going to happen, was going to happen, which made Adrian okay with that.

He was okay with a lot of things. Millie's way of looking at things made sense. It was logical. Of course sayings like, *it is what it is*, were perfect too, because what else would they be? Things cannot be what they aren't, only what they are. It was also Adrian's best way to deal with Joe.

Adrian felt that the way Millie treated the world, with acceptance, had started to rub off on him as well. It made him understand that it was not his fault that Joe was not open to talking with him, but rather, that Joe loved him in his own way. He learned it was good to speak to Joe, and that Joe's lack of responses didn't necessarily matter. Millie told him to view it as if he were inputting data into Joe's system.

He also felt that Joe must learn to deal with whatever came up, and Millie would be a successful part of this journey too. Even if he failed, it was going to be okay. The old Adrian would have been inundated with worry about Joe's failure at Albertsons. There were so many negative outcomes to future possibilities that Adrian would have been obsessed with, leading up to the grand cynical conclusion that Joe would never be able to function on his own and that he would always need them. Before he learned to be more accepting, Millie used to say that that was just Adrian being Adrian.

"And who else would I be?" he would laugh, knowing that a rare joke would go a long way with Millie.

With each successful number crunching, Adrian felt energized. He had so much control, and when he visited major cities on the travel cycle, with their tall buildings, he felt on top of the world. It was the complete opposite of the lack of control he felt when being passed around from different temporary parents as a child. With control came power, and when he had the power, he felt he was the best he could be.

Strangely, for a man with social anxiety, he loved New York City. New York City was a place he was energized by; he felt empowered by its size, both vertical and horizontal, yet he could still disappear into the masses of human chaos. Before he left on his trips there, he would show Joe his blue suit, and tell him that the day he wore it, he would be like Superman leaping tall buildings in a single bound. He would also show Joe pictures of tall buildings in New York, on Joe's America Online browser, uploading them one skinny pixelated line at a time, until they were complete.

The tallest one, he showed Joe, was the South Tower of The World Trade Center, where AON had offices on floors 92-105. When the elevators traveled upward, it gave Adrian a head rush which coincided with his growing feelings of power and confidence, increasing with each floor traveled. From the highest floor AON occupied, it was only five more floors up to the outside observatory, where Adrian would go on each trip to New York. Adrian could not believe how high he was, looking down at the rest of the world. It gave him a tingle in the pit of his stomach, a tingle which could have been either nerves or excitement. What a massive undertaking this building had been— and what a massive journey he himself had taken, going from a foster kid to the great life he had right now. He felt so high right at such moments that it would take something major to bring him down.

# Chapter Three

Joe's America Online screen name was *JoeSuperman767*. Joe used that ID to view subjects of interest, and to work on homework. The internet was wonderful for Joe, like an entire library in his bedroom. Adrian purchased America Online at first for Joe's benefit, as he himself had shown little interest in anything online, except for sending and receiving e-mail. Joe received e-mail too, but usually it was nothing except spam or mail from his mom, and dad. He responded to none of them, but generally appreciated his parents' efforts, especially the e-mail from his father, whom he was feeling less defensive around.

He also made a decision not to use America Online Instant Messenger, as *JoeSuperman767*, when he had other things to do. *JoeSuperman767* was a name which might give away his identity, which in turn, might cause conflicts if anyone recognized him as that. Conflicts were always in the forefront of his mind. Instead he used messenger as *TypicalAveragePerson767*, a user name he created and used to enter a few chatrooms.

The chatrooms confused him because they didn't seem real. No matter what the subject of interest was, the rooms all became either argumentative or sexual. It didn't make sense to him that when he wanted to chat about geology, someone wanted to know his age, location, and the size of his penis.

*TypicalAveragePerson767* was also the persona Joe used when he searched for, and found *GraceO'X15*, the screen name for Grace O'Halloran. *TypicalAveragePerson767* said his real name was Chase, and he went to a different school in Arizona, which was close by. As Chase, he was polite and interested in whatever Grace said, which was what he wanted things to be like if he actually spoke to her, in person, as Joe. Any time "Chase" would bring up his feelings of alienation, and not connecting to others, there was a long pause from Grace's end. He concluded that even when using a pseudonym, communication potentially caused unwanted results, so he continued only to respond to Grace, and kept it all in Grace's world. Mostly, he asked her questions about school. Still, he found it important to ask questions outside of that sometimes, in order to get her to open up. For example, while they were conversing about Biology, Joe asked what her favorite food was. By responding to her only in questions, he got information about Grace's relationship with Christopher. Joe found out she still loved him, but she didn't feel that this was going to last as a long-term relationship, and besides, she said, she was still young and wanted to experience more relationships than her first one.

Joe wanted to ask her if there were anyone else she had gone to junior high school with that she considering dating... maybe someone much quieter than Christopher? *No, not really*, she typed, *but I'll know when it happens*. Then she typed, *Thank you for being here. I really like chatting with you.*

Interactions like this tended to confuse Joe, not really sure if Grace's *no, not really*, was about how she felt about quiet people in general, or about him. He was using his own traits to talk about himself specifically, but was her answer specifically about him? It made him wonder if he could ever be Grace's boyfriend. Certainly there was a follow-up question he should have asked, but instead he typed, *I'm eating Cool Ranch Doritos. Do you like those better than the Nacho Cheese?*

# Chapter Four

After the Albertsons incident, no matter how painful it was to watch, Millie made sure neither she nor Joe were going to quit doing anything he needed to master, in order to eventually be out on his own. Joe told her that he understood the importance of these tasks, but he just had trouble completing them. Millie scaled back on the food shopping plan, decreasing the items, making sure Joe could successfully enter a store and then leave the store without any problems. The larger shopping part would need to be learned at a later date.

While Joe was learning independence, Millie noticed that Adrian had become more and more involved in Joe's life. It was more his scaling back on his micro-management and judgment which helped Joe to be more open to his father. Finally, after sixteen years, Adrian and Joe seemed to be developing a relationship. Joe appeared to miss his father when he went away. Who would have thought Adrian would have become the "good cop," in their relationship. Millie was more task and goal directed toward Joe, but she could do that. She had established Joe's trust at such an early age that she could be the one to push, even if playing that role did not fit into her personality type. Even her pushes in Laura's life were not as assertive, but they were finally being followed by her friend. Laura had hired a lawyer, borrowing the money from the Gamuts so Steven wouldn't notice anything missing from their bank account.

"Steven will have no idea," Millie told her, "and it will blow his mind, because he feels he has control over everything. But control can come crashing down when you least expect it," Millie added, taking a bite from her chicken salad sandwich while praying salmonella from the mayonnaise on a hot day wasn't growing between her slices of toast. "And then, what follows is pure panic."

"What about Adrian?" Laura asked. "Isn't he...?"

"Controlling? Adrian is more about control over his environment, for his own peace of mind. He doesn't really wish to control me, or even control Joe now, the way he used to. It is totally different. Plus, now things are better with us. I am even considering going on some of his business trips, not that I can right now, with Joe, but it's the thought."

"Why don't you? You always say that you miss the East Coast."

"I would like to visit New York, even if it seems so big. It's not like Boston at all, and Adrian thinks that the most romantic thing would be to have breakfast at the Windows On The World restaurant; but honestly, I'm a little scared of heights. Maybe, when Joe gets so he can stay on his own a bit more, I'll consider it."

"Well, after all you've done for me I could look in on him while you're away. I'm really so grateful to have you as a friend. I could never have done what I'm doing now without you."

"Oh, yes you could have. You're strong, Laura. You are a strong young woman, and you're doing what you need to be doing. And believe me, you are doing it!" Millie paused.

"Ha! You're not much older than me," Laura answered, brushing off the often maternal way Millie referred to her.

"As for New York ... perhaps, but not right now," Millie said, ignoring Laura's last statement. "Maybe, in a few years then. I mean, as it is, I don't see my own parents that much, so how can I justify going to New York?"

"You should do both," Laura said. "You're still an East Coast gal at heart."

"I feel I'm from there, but my temperament has changed, and is totally different from most East Coasters'. Adrian says I fit better out here because I'm just too nice a person for New York or Boston."

"I definitely am too," Laura said, as she jabbed a fork into her wilting salad. "I would miss the hot weather. You could fry an egg on this cement," she added. "Which helps when I feel like breakfast."

"Well, it's a good thing Adrian isn't here, because he would tell you that you couldn't do it, because he read about it, and it is proven that the sidewalks don't ever get that hot."

# Chapter Five

High school, as it turned out, wasn't as difficult a transition as Joe had thought it was going to be. His grades dipped a little, as participation and presentations were graded, which always brought down his average. Any written assignments produced a near perfect score, something his guidance counselor said she would write in a personal letter, to any dean of any college he applied to. Joe felt safe as a new sophomore at Sunnyslope High School, almost as if he fit in.

Joe also had insider information via "Chase" on Grace and Christopher's relationship issues, so when he observed them in the halls, he felt a little sad, knowing that soon Christopher's time with her would be up. Grace always made sure to say hello as they passed each other between classes, to which Joe answered, 'yes,' though he thought that maybe one day it would be different. One day he might say, 'hello,' too. In Joe's plan, when the big breakup occurred, he would try this bold switch, if there were no one else besides Grace within earshot to hear him say it.

Grace had some ideas about Joe as well. She had told her friends that if only Joe wasn't so eclectic, she might find him attractive. This wasn't met with any joshing from the girls, as Joe, it could be agreed, was very physically attractive. He had grown into a young man, with a physical build superior to his father, but with the same thin waist his father had. Joe also had more chiseled features than his mother had, but had her wide, strong shoulders. In the morning, he spent a lot of time on his appearance, making his hair neat, and styled with gel, mirroring a young Christopher Reeve. He also asked his mother to return the clothes which weren't at the level of the styles the popular kids at school wore, with the added difficulty that they also had to be soft, comfortable, and large enough to hide his security cape.

It took until November for Joe to receive the message. Posing as Chase on America Online, he knew that Friday was going to be the day of the breakup. Grace asked Chase for advice on the timing too. Should she wait until after the football game, so it wouldn't interfere with Chris's play? Chase told her that Friday would be a good time, because Christopher would have the weekend to think things out, and it would eliminate the next day drama at school. He also suggested she do it before the game, because there might not be time afterward, and then it would be a blown opportunity. Then he asked if she were officially single, to which she replied, *Are you wanting to ask me out?*

Joe did want to, but not as Chase, and certainly not as a new sophomore, because if it didn't work out, he would have more than a weekend, but rather three years, to feel strange about it all. Instead he answered in a way that he thought might be safe and intriguing, *Maybe I'll just show up at your school*, to which Grace did not type an answer, at all.

* * *

Christopher had the game of his life. Playing Defensive End, he was so wrapped up in anger about the breakup, he savagely stuffed every running play, and hurried, or sacked the quarterback on each pass play. He also raced across the field in such a rage, on an end-around play, that he viciously tackled the ball-carrying wide receiver, who was at least ten feet out of bounds. Upon contact, the relaxed runner, thinking the play was over, was launched into the Sunnyslope student wearing the Victor the Viking outfit, popping off the mascot's horned helmet, and shattering the poor Viking's femur.

# Chapter Six

Grace, who felt responsible for the mascot's broken leg, because of her raging ex-boyfriend, had accompanied the boy to the hospital, via an ambulance. The boy had just received the mandatory polite clap as he was loaded onto a stretcher and driven off the grounds, the siren blaring and the lights strobing against the dark Arizona night. Almost immediately, some of the parents in the stands worried aloud that if one of their sons were now injured, and there was no ambulance on hand to take care of their gladiator—what would happen? They feared it was dangerous to utilize an ambulance for an injured mascot, leaving their sons, the football players, vulnerable.

After the boy was placed in a cast, the staff at the Emergency Room asked him if he wanted his belongings in a bag. The belongings consisted of only the Victor the Viking outfit, which would have been too big to fit in a bag anyway. The boy paused, not really wanting to take it, as he didn't want to be reminded of the role responsible for his shattered leg. "Please take it, Grace. I never wanted to be the mascot to begin with," the boy moaned. "Are my parents coming?"

"I don't know. What's your name?" she asked him.

\* \* \*

The next afternoon, Grace arrived at 29 West Sunnyslope Lane holding a large Viking's head and its large fabric-and-plastic body in her hands. Joe was amazed she was there.

"I think this will be good for you, Joe," she said, holding out the mascot to the stunned Joe, who didn't put out his arms to receive it, allowing the outfit to fall at his feet.

"Oh, that's okay," she said, touching Joe on his shoulder, and moving closer to him.

"Yes," he responded, looking mostly at the ringlets of her hair, wishing his hands were engaged in her soft mane, as he thought about locking his lips, firmly, on what he imagined to be her soft ones.

"You can say, 'no,' if you want," she further probed, almost giggling, as she amused herself with the thought of Joe actually saying, 'no.'

"Yes," he said.

"I won't tell anyone. Your identity will stay hidden. This can be our secret, okay?" she said. Joe liked having secrets with Grace, but it was against his best instincts to accept the Victor the Viking costume. He knew already that when he wore it, it would never replace how he felt as Joe the Superhero. He wasn't sure if that was a good thing or a bad thing.

"You should get out more," she said before turning away. "You're very cute."

After she left, Joe went back to his room to privately work out his heightened feelings, and then walked back to the front door, still open, to grab the pile of Viking gear he'd left at the entrance. He might be able to pull it off, he thought, as he was not going to be Joe the Viking: he was going to be Victor. He also thought he might be able to present the mascot in a little bit more of a historical light, which he could impress Grace with.

Joe attempted to find a missing link between actual Vikings and Arizona. As much as he researched, though, he only found *potential* Viking settlements in eastern Canada and New England, and perhaps as far south as New York. Certainly, there were no Vikings in Arizona ever recorded in history. Joe thought maybe Victor was the great lost Viking, who was a bit of a renegade. But why would Victor have an urge to conquer or pillage the settlement at Sunnyslope High School? Victor the Viking only wanted to conquer or pillage Grace O'Halloran. Then he had an idea. If he was going to be a character, he would be a modern Viking, with the modern issues which faced people in the year 1999.

After seeing Joe with the costume, his mother tried to talk him out of it, knowing that there were things that might happen that Joe would not anticipate, even though he was going to be anonymous.

"I'm okay, Mom. If no one knows it's me, then I can do anything."

* * *

The last home game of the season was held traditionally on the final Saturday afternoon of November, instead of the usual Friday nights of games played during the season. Joe arrived as Victor, and no one asked him anything. Those in attendance just assumed that he was some dumb first year sophomore who got tricked into playing the part. Joe didn't want to be seen as such, as he was very defensive about being viewed as a dumb anything. He did recognize that in a way, he had been tricked.

Joe had planned on doing an act, as a Viking, which would be seen as pure brilliance. His Viking would be a mascot for all of society. Joe had brought a prop bag which had items symbolizing the problems of the modern world. In the first quarter, he brought out his computer keyboard, which was meant to represent the upcoming Y2K bug. He placed it on the team's bench, and started hammering away. Then he stood by the bench and leapt in the air as if he were blown up, acting out the terrorist bombing attack at two US Embassies in Nairobi and Dar es Salaam which had killed 250 people. *This is something worrisome in the modern world.* He thought at the least he would get the same polite clap that the previous Victor received for only breaking his leg, but his acting went unnoticed.

Then he moved on to health issues. He took a bottle of sunscreen which shielded against skin cancer, and spread it all over Victor. Unfortunately, the lotion remained white and clumped on the faux fur of Victor's chest. Joe had applied the white lotion as generously as recommended by the Surgeon General, and now there was lotion all over his costume. He was getting noticed, but the crowd, from what he could see and hear inside the oversized head, seemed to be laughing and pointing at him. Joe needed to turn the tide quickly, so for his final act, one he deemed to be serious enough to include in his show, he depicted Bill Clinton's sexual contact with Monica Lewinski. Joe, as Victor, covered in a white sticky substance, was now gesturing lewdly. He felt that people would understand that the lewdness he was representing was bad and inappropriate, and Joe, as it turned out, was correct. The parents completely viewed the act as bad and inappropriate, while the students found the lewd act to be comical.

When two police officers came over to roughly escort Joe back into the school, there was applause one hundred times louder than the previous mascot had received after his leg was broken.

\* \* \*

When the other students found out that Joe had been the mascot, his status peaked, but Joe, not realizing this, had not wanted to go to school the following Monday. There was a large amount of shame when his mother explained that his actions were interpreted as obscene. How could he disappear when he, as Victor, had thrown sunscreen around as if it were semen? His mother told him that no one had figured out it was a political statement about the Clintons.

When Monday came, he walked slowly down the edge of the hallways, head down, as he anticipated the bullying would begin. It never did. Instead, Joe received many pats on the back, some laughs, and a fan club dedicated to him, proposed by some of the marching band kids. It didn't seem to matter that Joe, playing Victor, had made lewd gestures while covered in white, sticky, sunscreen. The members of the student body thought it was hilarious, and so Joe was viewed as more normal than he had been just three days ago.

# Chapter Seven

When Laura came by a few days later, nearly in tears, Millie knew exactly what to do, as she had prepared herself for this day. *Damn if I'm not becoming more and more like my husband,* she thought, regarding her preparedness. Laura had a red mouse on the corner of her eye, which was going to become a shiner.

First, Millie asked her if she was safe, and she replied that she was now. Second, Millie cleared the area of all the men, sending Joe and Adrian to Joe's room, for what Millie called computer recreation time. After the mascot incident, she was more than happy for Joe to disappear in there for a few hours. Joe had needed more like a few days to feel he was in a safe haven; and Millie now needed to produce a safe place for Laura. It wasn't that Adrian and Joe, as men, were threats, but men's opinions, or even their presence, were not welcome right now. Millie also wanted some one-on-one time to be of service to her friend. After violence, and the fresh breakup of a marriage, it was important to suggest to her what a strong woman's role could be from this point on. First, Millie brought her an ice pack.

"Well the shit certainly hit the fan," Laura said, her voice deep as she struggled to make things light. "I've never seen him so angry. He kept shouting, 'Why are you doing this to me!'"

"Look, Laura, whatever you need right now from me, consider it available. You can even stay here for a bit until you get on your feet," Millie proposed.

"Thank you," she said. "But what should I be doing? Do I date? I don't really know how to date. Do I meet someone with my Yahoo? I've heard horror stories about meeting people on the Internet."

"One thing at a time," Millie said in a reassured manner. "Let's just do one thing at a time. First of all, do you want to press charges?"

"Oh, I don't know."

"I think it'll make you feel better. How about I drive you to the police station? We can file for a restraining order."

"Oh, those things never work. You should see some of my cases.... All the crazy ones in the world just ignore something like that, and they go out of their heads."

"I don't think Steven is crazy. Certainly not enough to be hospitalized."

"Steven IS crazy," Laura replied forcefully, her cross jaunting around her neck.

"Even if the restraining order works to just allow you to be able to go back and grab your stuff, I'm sure Sunnyslope's finest would be more than happy to help you out. Hey, wait!" Millie said, the information flying into her head, like the rush of an airplane's takeoff. "I know some of the officers because of...." Millie motioned in the direction of Joe's room. "A couple of them have even been nice to me," she laughed. "They are the ones that I've not yelled at, which in advocating for my son, leaves only a few."

"So, do you think they'll help?"

"I think so," Millie said, knowing that most likely the police would just tell her to file a restraining order anyway. "Let me make a call."

Ten minutes later, grizzled Officer Olson, and the much younger Officer Perkins, arrived at the door. Millie recognized the two as the ones who had driven Joe home in his Victor the Viking costume. Olson first asked how Joe was, informing her that he hoped he'd stayed out of trouble. "Joe is fine," she said, "but I didn't call you for that."

Even with Laura's swollen face and puffy eyes, the younger of the two officers kept looking up at her. He held his pen stiffly, his writing accelerating down his note pad, while questioning her. It was obvious enough for Millie to notice. *Well, even a bruised woman has sex appeal in her corner*, Millie thought, cynically, yet regretting the fact it was totally true. *Remember, officer, you're here because of a man, asshole. Don't think you're going to be next up.*

The young officer reached out to touch Laura on the shoulder, while suggesting a restraining order. Laura declined. "Well then, we can follow you and your friend to the house in the patrol car, so you can take everything out of there you need. It's not what we typically do...."

"Officer Perkins?" Olson said. "Can we talk for a minute?"

Perkins answered Olson confidently. "We were supposed to go to lunch anyway. We have time. Tell you what, Officer Olson. I'll buy you lunch after we help this young lady. I'll even buy you a coffee later. Deal?"

# Chapter Eight

Laura would never consider dating Officer Perkins, but after her ordeal, she did want to feel desired. She was glad to be driving by herself, followed by Millie plus a squad car, all heading to her house. She knew what Millie would talk about, and she was just too tired to engage. Yes, Millie was right, a strong woman should never need a man, but if Laura was honest with herself, she was in her late thirties now, and the benefit of her looks was not going to last too much longer, so she might as well use it while she still could. Deep inside, Laura felt that Millie was less worried about women being empowered for the wrong reasons, and more jealous that she had an advantage that God had given her, one that Millie never had. She tugged at the gold cross on her necklace, praying Steven wouldn't be home. *If looks are one of the things in my tool box I can use to empower myself, then what's so wrong with that?* Laura thought. *It's my choice.*

Steven wasn't home, so they packed up their cars quickly with some of Laura's belongings. After they were done, Officer Perkins leaned over the driver's side window, and asked Laura for her number, which she gave to him; but she knew she would never answer his calls.

\* \* \*

Although their faith had been tested by all of this, her parents, Paul and Mary Wellin, had a few guilt cards to play against their daughter. They could play the *the church doesn't approve of divorce, and you are a sinner* hand, which would morph into the self-righteous *I told you so before you ever got married* hand. What they said depended on what day it was or in what way they wanted Laura to feel bad. Laura knew the game well, because she grew up with it, and ultimately her self-image suffered for years before she figured out it was just a sick game her parents played to control her. All she knew was it was time to play Hide-and-Seek, for emotional survival, from both her parents and from Steven, and she knew 29 West Sunnyslope Lane was the place to do it.

* * *

Laura enjoyed her respite at the Gamuts. It was a good place to land from her toxic situation with Steven. She found that the nightly bottle or two of wine she used to need was no longer necessary. That was a part of her life she blamed Steven for. Yes, there were still nights she wanted a drink, and she had drunk excessively on the nights he was out—but drinking at home by herself had been eliminated since there was no reason for her to need the escape.

Laura lived at the Gamuts for half a year, and her presence also was beneficial to Millie, as it helped Millie get out of the house. Because of Laura, Millie had begun to travel with Adrian, coming back joyful and relaxed. Laura knew the truth would set Millie free, and the truth was that Millie was a very strong woman who enjoyed having time on her own to see the museums in New York or even the sights of Paris. Plus, it wasn't just Millie that had shown growth. It seemed that Joe was getting more independent without his mother micromanaging him, as he went to school on his own and even prepared his own meals. The only time Laura noticed him around was when he sought her out in a social way, but then Joe ended up standing there looking uncomfortable, with the same noticeable look Officer Perkins had given her, except with absolutely no game. Laura did not find it at all threatening, but almost complimentary in a strange way; Joe was a handsome young man, dark and attractive, his hair thick and stylish, his sideburns, difficult to ignore, long, shaped, and thin.

It looked like Joe had matured in the past six months, right in front of her eyes. Joe standing there wasn't at all like the other men who would check her out, because it was Joe, and she knew that it meant something different when Joe did things like that—unlike the other men, who made her feel like prey. She also knew, more than anyone else besides Millie, that Joe was one with a pure heart. *If only there was someone for me that had these same traits*, Laura thought. *Except they would have to talk more.* Then she pondered the spoken words of the recent men in her life, and thought, *well, perhaps not.*

# Chapter Nine

Millie had started classes part-time at Arizona State University at Tempe, just about the time Joe entered his junior year at Sunnyslope High. It was the same college Laura had attended when she switched her job focus from maternity to psychiatric nursing. The classes were at night, but she felt at ease leaving Joe home alone while she was attending to her degree.

One afternoon, she sought out a counselor at their education offices, to discuss Joe, more specifically, how he would function at college, if he were to attend here too. Shortly after, she and Joe went on a visit, so he could see what college was all about, and perhaps want to go there as well. Maybe, she thought, Joe would apply there, and if they remembered him, it might open the door. Millie thought the idea of both of them in college at the same time was pretty exciting, and both of them at the *same* college, full-time, would be convenient, functional, and of course, sensational. Adrian didn't need the emotional side of the plan to sell him on it, but he too felt Joe and Arizona State would be a perfect fit.

Millie also visited the employment offices at Arizona State, as she and dependent children of employees at Arizona State would have 50% reduced tuition. The word "dependent child," gnawed at her stomach, even though it was being used differently by definition. She wondered what she could do for employment in a university environment. She didn't have a high enough degree to teach, and her Psychology degree, earned at Boston University, opened few doors for her. Food service was out of the question. Then she saw a bulletin board listing for Child Care Specialist at the Children's Center, to work with children aged 1-5. She dropped off an application for full-time work at close to minimum wage.

If Joe hadn't been comfortable enough to occupy himself at home, this wouldn't have been an option. Now, leaving Joe on his own would be a natural way to encourage his independence. She envisioned him cooking dinner for himself, or maybe Adrian, and learning a day-to-day routine that was more than his current school, homework, and computer time. Joe had aced all the at-home tasks Millie had wanted him to master. This was easy for him, as Joe's problems never happened at home, but out in the community when he needed to interact.

To Millie's surprise she was called in for an interview on the next day. A young HR person, whom Millie couldn't imagine being much older than her own son, liked the fact that she was older than all the students who currently worked there as a part of the work-study program. He looked uncomfortable in his white dress shirt and tie costume. He suggested that they were looking for a nurturing, maternal presence at the center, because the children there had overly busy mothers who worked or went to school, or both; hence their need for child-care during the day. "You would be the elder-matriarch of the center," he added, stretching his neck for freedom from his confining, button-down, white collar.

Millie felt that much of what he said about matriarchal nurturing was pretty off base, borderline sexist, and grounded in stereotypes. She had always thought of herself as efficient, liberal, and certainly out of the box; at least she was for her generation. *Nurturing, maternal, and gasp, elderly? We'll just see about that.*

Finally, after putting up with the HR screener, Millie was given a tour of the facility. A day care associated with Arizona State, rather than being a private center, certainly had its advantages, Millie noted. Everything there was new—the toys, the carpet, the sofa. Visually, it was pretty amazing. The kids even looked freshly pressed out of a JC Penney catalog. The boys, in their IZOD shirts and cargo shorts, were bouncing balls or rolling cars and trucks on the floor of the large classroom. Their cubbies featured life-sized images of Phoenix Suns and Arizona Cardinals players. The girls all were gathered around a toy kitchen area. A few were noticeably happy and shouting as they played at a gargantuan doll house. The staffer she was going to be supervised by was a blonde woman named Tiffany, a junior, who was majoring in Child Development, Class of 2002. Tiffany reminded Millie of a young Laura, and when Millie was introduced, she told

Tiffany that she would only work for her if the center focused on
producing strong women, and for that matter, stronger men, who
respected women. Tiffany held on to Millie's handshake for a much
longer time than usual; and when her head turned to the young HR
officer, her eyes pleaded, "We must hire this woman."

# Chapter Ten

By his junior year, the notoriety of the mascot incident had faded, but Joe's reputation as someone you didn't expect to be pretty cool, but was, was left intact. His classmates left him pretty much to his own devices, except Grace had invited him, immediately after his Victor act, to sit with her and her friends, which he still did. What he didn't still do was interact with her as Chase, mostly because Grace had gotten sick of America Online Instant Messenger, and Joe couldn't figure out a way to connect with her in real life, as Chase, even when Grace had suggested they actually meet.

Laura had only stayed at the West Sunnyslope Lane house until she and Steven settled their divorce. He got the house, but she was able to buy a house of her own, about forty-five minutes outside of Phoenix, in Apache Junction, where U.S. Route 60 meets the Apache Trail. Joe still saw her every few weeks, but he missed their daily interactions and missed being close enough to take in her light floral scent, and later, fantasize in his bedroom about what it would be like to be with her.

When she came by, Laura took Joe on her rounds, visiting Shades, who was always planning the next festival and how to make it better. Shades referred to them as "Laura and her man," which Joe thought was encouraging, and Laura only laughed at.

"I hope to never have to have a man at all," she said. "I'm much stronger by myself"—a claim which Joe didn't think was encouraging, so he focused on his favorite costume, always here, never rented, very reliable.

But Joe knew something different about Laura and men, as he had eavesdropped on her conversations from behind his partially closed bedroom door. He heard that Laura was dating, but only casually, and occasionally having casual sex—then immediately breaking off contact with the guy before he became obsessed with her. Joe would often hear his mother say either that she was envious of the freedom of that arrangement, or that she couldn't ever do what Laura was doing. The two opposites confused Joe into thinking about whether what she was doing was bad or good. Joe noted that his mother, even though conflicted about it, didn't seem disapproving, so all must be fine.

# Chapter Eleven

Millie now traveled with Adrian on 25% of his AON business trips, an increase of around 15%. The rate had started at around 10% when Laura still lived with them and Millie was able to take time off from her job, usually when Arizona State was on its college breaks, and the day care was closed. Adrian enjoyed that she came with him, because, even though she was on her own, taking in her favorite spots at her favorite locations, it indicated the desire to do things with him. Places like Aruba, Boston, New York, or London, England were always a 'yes,' but Millie could do without traveling to Fort Worth, Texas, or the other London, the one located in frigid Ontario.

It didn't matter to Adrian where he was sent, and AON knew Adrian was all business, so he often got sent to the less glamorous sites. It was perfect for his less glamorous wardrobe which consisted of three black suits, seven white shirts, seven undershirts, his dress shoes, and a rotation of proper looking ties. Adrian was always sent to New York City because it was one of their biggest offices, one which took care of important world business accounts. On those trips he added his blue suit and his Superman-garnished necktie to his garment bag. One day he would like Joe to join him and Millie there, and he would take some time off to walk him around the city, to show him all the skyscrapers. He knew Joe would enjoy and appreciate New York City, but the challenge would always be producing a safe enjoyment versus the exciting stimulation of a place like downtown Manhattan. His son preferred visiting the places where Adrian was currently situated via his computer, checking out each location's images, and viewing the hotels and restaurants his father e-mailed him about.

Whenever he worked in Los Angeles, or San Francisco, Adrian had a strange feeling, deep in his stomach, when it was sunny, or calm and without any breeze. He knew that when the weather was warm and the air felt dead, there was a greater chance of an earthquake. He also remembered the big Bay Area earthquake of 1989, which happened when Joe was still a small child. *Hadn't the weather been perfect that day? Yes. It had been the kind of weather that people moved to California for.* It made Adrian worry about the potential connection between calm, beautiful, weather, and disasters.

Then, last week, before a Los Angeles trip, he had been on America Online, showing Joe AON's downtown buildings; that search somehow took him to The United States Geology Survey, which informed them that there is no greater chance of an earthquake occuring during calm or sunny weather. Adrian had been wrong, which unnerved him as a man who ran his life on numbers and probabilities. It was actually major storm systems such as tropical cyclones—not the warmer, calmer days associated with low-pressure systems—that induced fault slips and, in turn, earthquakes.

So they looked up avalanches, and they found that when temperatures are at their lowest, snowfall sticks to the surface. When temperatures increase, snow will slough off and slide down a slope. Any number of disturbances, including loud noise or a skier's motion, can cause an avalanche. With these facts came photos and videos, which would pause as they uploaded them, of buildings collapsing, with giant waves of snow cascading from a mountain's upper peaks down to the ground.

Something in those internet pages made Adrian feel restless and uneasy. Certainly, his trip to Los Angeles would be fine, and he probably was just having a visceral reaction to viewing disturbing images on the computer. *Feelings are not facts*, he thought, as he reminded himself that he'd taken tons of trips all over the world and had never experienced any natural disasters that had put his life at risk. Then he thought about his son, Joe, whose very mind caused natural disasters internally for him on a day-to-day basis, depending on his level of anxiety. Adrian gasped, wondering why he himself seemed to be having such a case of high anxiety, especially when things were better than they had ever been.

Thinking about how good his life was, and a big deep breath, had him feeling temporarily better, but there was another odd occurrence which reversed everything once again. Right after an image of the

1989 San Francisco earthquake filled the monitor, with one of people stuck in the rubble, Joe moved his mouse to shut down the computer, which then spoke to them with a flat emotionless, 'goodbye,' to which Joe answered, 'yes,' while looking at his father. Joe's interaction with the machine, which confirmed the finality of the shut-down, made Adrian feel even more nervous than he had felt when he was viewing the actual photos of death and disaster. There was something strange and eerie about this particular good-bye, and to further confirm this feeling, after his son said goodbye to America Online, he leaned over to Adrian, and for maybe the first time ever, initiated a hug.

* * *

Adrian had noticed Joe had been doing really well when he was left home alone. At first, Laura had been there to ease him into the idea of being less dependent. Then when it was time for Joe to fly solo, Adrian half expected the house to be in shambles upon his return, or Joe to have had some incident where there was police involvement. Adrian knew if that were to happen there was a chance he and Millie wouldn't find out he was in custody, because 'yes,' is not a phone number, and more importantly, Laura was now forty-five minutes away, not close enough to monitor the situation. Millie scolded Adrian for his worry, especially if, when he was away, he initiated a random call to the police station to see if Joe was being held there. Millie hated the police, and she told Adrian that *if he kept being a pain in the ass, the police would not be easy on Joe or the family if they ever were to be involved.*

AON's annual family-friendly trip in 2001 was to occur in New York in early September. Adrian was planning that, for this event, both Millie and Joe would be joining him. Adrian knew if Joe worked at something, or had a long enough time to process information, he would function much better when the time came to participate. That, and some of Millie's desensitization techniques, which helped, would be needed for this plan to come to fruition. Adrian couldn't shake his anxiety, as it grew closer, and closer to that September date. If only he could come up with a logical conclusion about this, or understand why he felt such a sense of impending doom.

# Chapter Twelve

Laura remembered watching the movie, *Looking for Mr. Goodbar*, as a child, and then having nightmares about it. She reasoned that Theresa Dunn, the school teacher in the movie, got what she deserved because what she was doing was morally wrong. Laura's mother told her that even watching the movie was morally wrong, and against church teachings. Now, as an adult, she knew it would not be easy to go home with random people, even if she wanted, because she feared, like in the movie, the last one would kill her. Still, there was something about being safe, always using a condom, knowing who you were taking home, and not being stabbed to death, which appealed to her. She felt blessed to have a sex drive, after virtually having none with her husband, which overtook the fear, and allowed her to enjoy herself, but, of course, with caution. She had exaggerated a few extra encounters for Millie's benefit, just so Millie would think she was freer and more empowered than she was.

In truth, initially she went out a few times in her new hometown, Apache Junction, went home with a couple of men, and decided that neither dating nor sex with no strings attached was right for her. The men all seemed to want some kind of commitment the times she didn't want any; or they ran if she did. The whole scene made her feel lonely.

Recently, there was a man she'd worked with that she took home after they had gone out for drinks. There was something kind and a little shy about him. He seemed like a guy who would be an enjoyable addition to her life. She was impressed by how he interacted with the patients and how he honestly seemed into her. After they arrived at Apache Junction, things went well, and she agreed to drive him home in the morning. The next day, she was more surprised than he was when she saw some of his clothes had been left outside his house *by his wife*, their colors bleaching out in the hot sun. She had thought that she had actually found a nice guy, a man who wasn't covered in the typical cheating, lying, abusing, male slime. How wrong she had been.

Besides the dating or near dating she was doing, Laura enjoyed living in Apache Junction, a town Adrian used to pass through on his way to Legend City. The town was your typical Arizona desert town, with big cactus all around, and mountains to the North East. She liked being near the Superstition Mountains, because there was always something magical about superstitions. It also was a federal wilderness area and home of the Lost Dutchman's Gold Mine. On the east border were the Goldfield Mountains, and the city of Mesa lay on the west. Apache Junction offered a great housing value, mostly because it was close to the airport. She purchased a nice three bedroom in Apache Junction, using one bedroom for potential guests, and the other extra one for an office. Even the commute to work didn't seem so bad, as she was driving a new car. She had acquired Steven's recently bought BMW in the divorce, but she immediately traded it in: a mid-sized Nissan was good enough.

She loved taking Joe with her because he loved to see the Goldfield Ghost Town, a tourist location preserved from former prospecting days, near the western face of Superstition Mountain, just off Highway 88. She'd thought he wouldn't enjoy a place like that, touristy with loud fake gunfights. The wilderness area seemed to be more his pace. But as time went by, she noticed that Joe seemed to jump at the chance to go anywhere with her.

# Part VI

# Chapter One

On the second weekend in September of his senior year, Joe didn't jump at the chance to go to New York with his parents on the AON family trip, even though he wanted to. His dad pleaded and showed him images on the computer, and even thought that one of Joe's 'yesses' was enthusiastic enough to actually be a 'yes.' Joe knew that it was important for his dad to "take the family to New York," on AON's annual family week, but he felt nervous: there was something in that large mass of people that wouldn't go right. It was a long trip, and something about being on an airplane, flying into New York, caused him to retreat. Adrian kept pushing, because the only time Joe had ever gone on the company event was the year Family Week was held in Phoenix.

His mom had been pushing him too. It had started a few months ago, and part of the desensitization plan was to walk around the business district in Phoenix during busy lunchtime. The walk never materialized, as either Joe or his mother was at school, or she was at work. The one time they tried in the summer, it was over 100 degrees, and the crowd stayed inside their air-conditioned buildings. Joe knew his dad could have manipulated his typical reply, and taken him to New York, but it was his mother, the trusted empathetic listener, the one he could talk to, who said the final 'no' which he couldn't say for himself. It was four weeks into his senior year, so logically, going away for a week in September made little sense. His parents left without him and agreed to document their trip through their words and pictures on e-mail. On the evening of September 10, Joe received his first one. It was from his father. It was full of facts, but no pictures.

*Dear Joe,*

*Your mother and I arrived in New York via Los Angeles where
the flight first had to land, to transfer to the American Airline
767 to New York. We arrived on Sunday September 9 and
promptly got stuck in a traffic jam of tennis fans near Flushing
Meadows, where Lleyton Hewitt had just won the US Open.
Today, we visited the Empire State Building and used our 'Superpasses', supplied by AON. A Superpass includes a lot of
tourist activities, at no charge, such as the observation deck
at the World Trade Center. We needed 'Superpasses,' or Superman, to get up there, because your mom and I can't fly. It
is a fairly hazy day, so we decided to wait for a clearer day to
visit the WTC. We decided on breakfast. Your mother is not
looking forward to sitting way up there, but it is my tradition,
which I look forward to sharing with her. It's quite interesting
being up there. Your mother might be afraid of heights, but
she'll never admit that she is weak on anything. I'll be wearing
the blue suit, and will try to send pictures tomorrow.*

*Your father,*

*Adrian Gamut*

Very concrete, Joe thought, noticing the e-mail read like a news
report, which was good since anything which included emotions
would confuse him, as it certainly would his father. Even the slight
break from the factual, in the e-mail, the obvious dad joke about
needing a 'Superpass,' or Superman to get to the Observation Deck,
was lost on him. *What was the connection, as earlier in the e-mail his
dad wrote about airplanes, and now he was making a Superman joke,
where flying and the World Trade Center were mentioned?* Joe starting
making the flying noises, out loud, a very unusual occurrence when
no one was around.

When he stopped, he was able to focus on genetics. His Biology
class at Sunnyslope High taught him all about dominant and recessive
genes. To Joe, it seemed that his father's lack of emotional genes,
and abundance of nut and bolt genes, had been passed to him, at one
hundred times the intensity. Joe observed his mother trying to fix
his father in ways different from the ones she used when fixing him.
Having his father send the e-mail rather than his mother was part of
the work in progress, although 'Adrian Gamut' signed off on the news
report like an anchorman.

His mother always sent the far more descriptive and interesting e-mails. They would include the color, make and model of their rent-a-car, where they were staying, who they sat next to on the flight, etc., etc., etc., while his father's would always include a report about the weather. Her e-mails helped him visualize things in his mind, as that was an area extremely lacking in Joe's makeup. Since the e-mail was from his father, he didn't write back. Joe had school the next day, so he shut down his computer and went to bed.

\* \* \*

Adrian had an omelet, toast, and coffee, and Millie had her eggs over easy that morning. Adrian's personal routine was an 8:00 breakfast, before taking the elevator all the way down the North Tower, and then up the South Tower, to report to work. This day, he started his routine later than usual. After all, it was Family Week at AON, and he was having breakfast with his wife. The restaurant was more crowded today, filled with AON employees. The air was still, and the day was sunny and calm. Then, the building shook. They were told to stay where they were. The restaurant filled with smoke. Within minutes there was an addendum to the plan, to try to get out. Then they were told, again, to stay where they were, help was on the way.

# Chapter Two

It was only a month into Joe's senior year when it happened. Typically for seniors, the year flew by quickly, For Joe, it turned into the slowest year ever, a painful crawl which started on September 11th. On that morning, televisions were turned on in all classrooms. Period 0 started at 7:00 a.m., and the South Tower fell one minute after the sound of the bell. Students sat in stunned silence: some of them were crying, and Joe was producing a low noise of flying, which he needed to soothe himself. He used all of his strength and control to not produce any loud noises or behaviors, which would force his removal from the classroom. He couldn't look away, though he wanted to. He needed to see his father. He looked for the blue suit. Joe knew his father worked in the South Tower, because he had shown him the on-line pictures of where he worked in the tall metropolis.

Then, during a replay of some of the events, he saw him. The news shifted to a helicopter shot of the North Tower. People were jumping. Joe felt he needed to fly. He wished they all could fly. If his father could fly, he'd be alright. After all, his talk about his blue suit perhaps was a hint that he really knew how to do something which Joe only fantasized about.

But, there his father was, hanging on the edge of one of the windows. He was small on the screen, in his blue suit, and holding onto him was his mother. Joe tried to grasp it, his parents in peril on the North Tower. It didn't make much sense, as Joe knew his father worked in the South Tower, but there he was in his unique blue suit. His mother wore a white cotton top, which billowed out from the wind, and then more so, after they stepped off the building and into the air. Joe couldn't see details but he hoped his father was not wearing his glasses. That was the only hope for survival. There was no time for Clark Kent in a scene like this.

If there were any miracles in Joe's reality, the television news would have featured his father and mother, in their blue and white blended colors, like Superman and Lois Lane, together, in the air, in an act of love. They'd be flying.

This wasn't the case. There was nothing Joe, his mother, his father, or anyone could do. None of them could fly, and no one could be saved. The certainty of it all was there were no superheroes, and no one in the world can fly. No one.

Joe stood up; pulled off his hidden cape from under his shirt; and made the loudest scream he had ever made. It was not the sound of Superman's flight, but rather the horrifying sound of shock. His classmates had no idea that Joe was howling at the specific loss of his parents, not viscerally reacting to the horrible sight of all the people jumping to their deaths from the height of over one hundred stories. Joe much later would recall Grace approaching him to calm him, then wanting to stop himself from pushing her; but there was nothing he could have done to control himself from shoving her away, and on to the ground. His sensory overload had determined that she was not coming to console him, but rather she was approaching quickly, and dangerously, to crash into him. The next thing he remembered, he was no longer at school, and there was loud knocking at the door of his house.

# Chapter Three

After ringing the bell repeatedly, Laura banged hard and loud at the door of 29 West Sunnyslope Lane. There was no answer. She drove to the school, but they did not know Joe's whereabouts either. They told her he became upset watching the news, and he shoved a student to the ground and ran out of the school. Laura told the school administrative assistant that Joe's parents were in New York, and his father was working in the South Tower. She had tried to call them, but their cell service in New York City was down.

Laura thought about calling the police, because she was more and more frantic, and too upset to keep going by herself. It might be better if the police handled the wellness check on Joe, instead of her. They could break down the door, if necessary. Then she remembered that there was a possibility that Officer Perkins might take the call, and the last thing she wanted was Perkins, or any man, hitting on her at a time such as this. She also knew that since Joe was 18, and a legal adult, able to make his own decisions, the police would not waste their time on a day so tragic.

Laura decided that if she couldn't do anything, and the police were as useless as she imagined, perhaps she just needed to be home by herself to grieve, be angry, or feel whatever she needed to feel. All she wanted to do right now was to escape. Intermittently, she had some hope that maybe Adrian and Millie hadn't gone for breakfast at the top of The World Trade Center this morning. Maybe, even, there was a chance that Millie was alive and she just couldn't reach her; after all, cell phone service was down. Then, she thought some more. *Didn't Adrian always stick to his schedule, leaving for work before the plane would have hit, and didn't Millie complain about him always wanting to take her to The Windows On The World restaurant? Maybe they'd left before the strike and were safe. Maybe they had gone to a different restaurant?* Laura then remembered how important it was to Millie to try to adjust to Adrian's day-to-day inflexibilities, as it would relax him and make him not feel anxious. *Maybe today, while on vacation, she didn't care about adjusting. Maybe things were alright.*

Laura, without any luck in resolving this conflict, drove back to Apache Junction, turned on the news recapping the event, and hit her knees. She held her gold cross necklace in her hands, like a rosary, repeating the Hail Mary, and the Our Father, again and again, but the planes kept hitting the buildings, again and again, and the buildings kept falling down. She prayed that the Gamuts would be alright. She prayed that she would be alright. And she prayed that everything, and everyone, would be alright. The sun outside her home was so bright that the light flowing through the window hurt her eyes, but she was afraid to get up mid-prayer to close the blinds.

Then she prayed harder than ever that New York wasn't a real place, had never been a city, and was only a vacant place, like the area of Arizona where she lived. She prayed it was not the huge target of a city, only an island covered in sand and cactus. She wished New York City was so unappealing that terrorists would say, *no, not this vacant place with just cactus and sand. No, not today, nor not ever.* If God could answer her prayers, then things would be alright, and none of this would have actually happened.

\* \* \*

Laura woke up on the floor, and it was dark outside. The television was still on; the news had still taken place. She had brought herself to a peaceful sleep while praying and creating a world where there was no such thing as people dying in mass numbers. In this world things were not important enough for people like Adrian and Millie to die for. Her necklace was still in her hands, the cross resting in her palms. She remembered a few years ago, Steven accusing her of not being a person that really believed or lived her life according to the teachings of Jesus. He had said she shouldn't wear her necklace because of that, but it had only made her want to wear it more prominently, perhaps giving it more power to ward off his evil. But today, she had a tough time with the belief that there was a loving God, when so many people who were only working or eating breakfast could be killed. She went to the sink to get a glass of water and wondered whether, if she tossed her necklace into the garbage disposal, perhaps things would all be changed. She flipped the switch, water running down the sink, and held the necklace by its thin chain, over the drain, watching as it swayed. She stood there for what felt like ten minutes, but perhaps was only a few seconds, then switched her grip from the chain to the cross of her necklace, and shut off the disposal. She did not want to completely destroy her faith; she decided, instead, to do something else. She opened the kitchen drawer, the one that was filled with string, scraps of paper, rubber bands, a few cigarette lighters, twist ties, and thumb tacks. Then, she threw her necklace in with the junk, took her car keys off the counter, and drove to the liquor store.

# Chapter Four

The reading of the Gamuts' Last Will and Testament was only attended by Richard and Samantha Englander. They stood there stoic, as they had released all of their crying while still in Massachusetts and on the flight over. Adrian and Millie had left everything to Joe. The small house at 29 West Sunnyslope Lane, which he had always felt comfortable in, hadn't had a mortgage in years. Adrian's investment money, which Millie would have received most of, was now fully inherited by Joe in a trust, which named Laura as a trustee if neither he nor Millie could assume that role. The fact that she had seemingly disappeared too didn't matter much; the will had been written before he turned eighteen, and Joe, at his age, no longer needed a trust or a trustee.

Richard and Samantha in their grieving had stopped speaking over one another. Their conversations were slow, sad, and deliberate. At times, their house in Cambridge had been silent.

"Is there anything in there about Joe going into a group home or foster care?" Richard asked.

The Gamuts' lawyer pondered the question, and then replied, "Well, since he is of legal age, and there is no documented disability, neither case would apply."

"We can't pack up and move here, and certainly Joe wouldn't be able to live with us in Cambridge," Samantha confessed. "What does apply in this case?"

"Joe should be financially set on his own," the lawyer answered. "There are no provisions, except for the inheritance, which should be satisfactory for a person to live on for a good long time."

"Is there any way to contact this Laura... Laura...?" Richard stumbled on her name.

"Wellin," the lawyer said, finding the last name on the document. "I tried to contact her before today's reading, and even sent someone to her last known address, but we have been unable to locate her." Suddenly, the Englanders were back in their comfortable cadence of conversation.

"Well, he is eighteen," Richard said.

"And he's about to finish school," added Samantha.

"And he has grown in independence, according to what Millie said."

"He uses an ATM..."

"He shops..."

"Well, sort of..."

"And, he occupies himself, S..."

"That Wellin woman will be back, R, she's a family friend..."

"I know, she'll be back...."

And, as they alternated, the Gamuts' lawyer wondered how the couple could keep up with their conversation, as they were, once again, speaking over one another. Richard and Samantha had, for the first time since 9/11, fallen into their rhythmic, comfortable pattern of speech.

"And if a worst case scenario happens," Samantha said, "I'm sure we'll be notified." And as it always happened, the end of their conversation broke away from chaotic communication to absolute stillness.

# Chapter Five

Joe no longer believed there was comfort found within his Superman alter-ego, so, after ripping the terrycloth cape off himself at school, he never replaced it. He would have to learn to take care of his anxieties, from the day-to-day stressors to the day-to-day routines, the best way he could, or suffer the consequences if he couldn't.

Joe knew he would never see his parents again, yet he hoped they were still alive, somewhere in the rubble. Sixteen had escaped from Stairwell B, in the North Tower, so perhaps, however remote the chance was, there were other pockets of life to be found in the collapsed towers. He checked online for any news, or recent developments, refreshing the browser, over and over again, so that he couldn't leave his house, waiting until he had the answers. All he found were hideous pictures of the buildings on fire, them falling, or the wreckage of the Twin Towers. He stopped going to school. Occasionally, there were knocks on the door, but there was no reason to open it. Joe was completely alone.

Isolating himself, Joe's mind started to play tricks on him. What if his parents weren't even in New York, but they just wanted to hide and not come home? Joe dialed the work number and extension of his father's office, but no one picked up. He called his mother's job, but someone picked up that was not his mother, and said, "Hello..., Hello..., Hello...," a few times before hanging up. When he called back again, he answered each 'hello" with a 'yes' until they demanded, "Don't you have better things to do?" They'd thought it was a prank.

Joe felt lost. If his parents were dead, where was Laura? Where were his grandparents? Joe wasn't dumb, he knew first hand that people handled stressful or catastrophic situations differently. Perhaps they all were hiding. Joe's powerlessness was causing him to feel helpless, so he knew he had to make an attempt to look for his mother. He decided he would walk to Arizona State University and find her.

The walk took five hours. He walked south on Route 51, staying as far off to the side as he could, to not be noticed. He walked past various estates and developed neighborhoods. He even walked past the address of the old Legend City location, which made him sad. If that place only still existed, maybe his father would still be.... He stopped, then cursed himself for even thinking it. *Working? Alive?* he thought. *Wasn't I making this walk with the hope that he would still be alive?*

When he arrived where his mother worked, it was the early afternoon, and the children were sitting in a circle being read to. One was sitting on the lap of a young blonde student, who was their teacher. They had snacks and cups, and they were being cared for the way a mother cared for their child; but he did not see his mother in the group. There was a crayon drawn picture of his mother on poster board, bordered in red, white, and blue. There were words written neatly by an adult, which read, "Never Forget," and "Always in Our Hearts—We Will Miss You, Mrs. Gamut." Joe's usually groomed appearance was sweaty from his long walk, his skin red and splotchy from the sun, his body drooping. The girl looked up, then stopped reading as Joe stood in front of her and the children. He did not know what to do, but in that moment he wanted to reverse time back to when he was young, and being cared for, by his own mother, or by Laura. They used to read to him too. Joe sat down in the circle with the children, wanting to magically change his wishes to reality, but the reading had now stopped, and the girl who had been reading looked apologetic, and her eyes looked wet.

"Hello, Joe," she said. "Boys and girls, this is Mrs. Gamut's son."

# Chapter Six

Laura felt that her friend Millie was not a strong woman. She discovered this during the second stage of the five stages of grief; but why, when she had finally reached acceptance, did the anger continue? When she woke from nightmares in the middle of the night, she found herself screaming. In the morning, she asked God–why hadn't he taken her instead of Millie? And why hadn't Millie been as strong as Laura had resolved her to be? *If Millie had been a strong woman, she would have asked for a breakfast location that SHE, not HE, found romantic. Maybe breakfast in bed would have been appropriate. Then they could have watched the news on that day in bed, and felt as powerless and sad as I have been feeling ever since, but without losing someone they loved,* she thought. *If Millie had been a strong woman, she would still be alive,* was her conclusion—supported by her feelings, which were not facts.

*Strong women run from bad/abusive relationships*, Laura thought, but the avoidance she was doing now was just running in disguise, and if she stopped to think, she felt a lot of guilt for not being strong herself. Right now, life in general seemed impossible, so coping day-by-day, hour-by-hour, was all she had. There was also the guilt of knowing Joe was out there without his parents. If only she could be there for him; but she wasn't in the best of shapes, not being able to take care of herself, much less him.

Laura was lost. She didn't know where she was running to, only from, but she knew that when things felt better, she planned to return to as normal a life as possible. She drank daily, so somehow it never felt she was going to get to that normal place. She had little hope, and the days became months. Spiritually, she was as bankrupt as the two-bit gamblers she ran into one night in Las Vegas, and then hung out with for months. Mail arrived at the Apache Junction residence, and after six months the foreclosure on her house began; but by that time, she was in San Francisco.

San Francisco, after her jaunt to Vegas, seemed slightly like a step closer to God, as Vegas had seemed like Satan's jungle to her. In San Francisco, she got a small job at a Methadone clinic, which kept her alive. San Francisco, full of transient people who, she was told, were not to be confused with homeless people. Laura considered herself transient, not homeless, during this escape.

There were some other things which worked in her favor. California belonged to the Nurse Licensure Compact, an agreement that recognized the licenses of nurses to practice in multiple states. Since San Francisco was so transient, she never had to change her primary residence, though she'd need to transfer her nursing license quickly if she did; so, she never did.

At least, along the way, she hadn't tried to solve her problems by being taken care of by a man, although there were plenty of offers to take care of her, in some way or another. Her problems had quickened the loss of her youthful appearance, the one where she always looked ten years younger than she was. But she no longer cared about having that tool in her toolbox. She knew that with a man, maybe, and initially, she would be taken care of, but her own problems wouldn't be solved, and more likely they would increase. She hadn't discovered that same truth about alcohol, about how it increased, rather than solved, her problems...yet.

# Chapter Seven

It was Joe who needed to summon the strength to use the tools he had learned so he could survive on his own. People like young Tiffany, from The Child Center could not help with that. She knew *of* Joe, from conversations with his mother, but had not actually met him until that day when she let him stay and listen. She had the opportunity to be kind, and she took it. She would have liked to have said something to him, but when day care ended, Joe got up and left, like a ghost being seen for one split-second before disappearing.

Joe, without knowing, had received some secret help from Grace O'Halloran. She had been the one who persistently knocked on Joe's door, almost daily, hoping that one day he would be up for letting her in. Behind the scenes, she had been advocating for him, against the school, to allow him to graduate, based on "special circumstances." One of her arguments was that other classmates with greater disabilities received high school diplomas, and they intellectually tested at only a grade school level; in fact, some couldn't read or write at all. Joe, on the other hand, was working at a college level, and certainly had shown himself to be highly intelligent and worthy of attending Arizona State University. Grace had filled out an application for Joe. Now, he needed a high school diploma and an additional letter from Sunnyslope High School, to explain the "Incomplete" grades listed for every one of his classes senior year. Grace kept digging in until she got them.

Then Joe, seemingly out of the blue, received an acceptance letter from Arizona State University. It seemed too overwhelming. How would he get there? It was a five-hour walk, and even if classes began in six months, the task seemed impossible. The knocks on his door kept coming, but answering them was impossible too, as there was going to be a person behind the knock, and he couldn't possibly deal with them. Even walking to Albertsons and purchasing food, in order to subsist, was an iffy activity. Sometimes, even when there wasn't food in the house, Joe was still unable to bring himself to leave and buy some. Many times, it wasn't until he was absolutely weak with hunger, that he would force himself, with a head full of anxiety, to make the trip, often running in to grab non-targeted items from his list. The cans of tuna he wanted would come home as cans of chicken spread. Instead of orange juice, Joe would capture Sunny-D. Cottage Cheese replaced yogurt, and so on. He didn't even like those items.

The market was easier in the early morning hours, after midnight, but best at 4 a.m. He reasoned that, to decrease interactions, he would shop at the 24-hour Albertsons at that hour. Although it was less crowded, Joe was still wary of the late-night clientele who seemed sketchy and potentially dangerous. What if they were drunk, or strung out on something, and needed to rob him for money? The constant conflict between reducing anxiety versus eating—choosing the best possible time to be out of his house—was always being battled in his head.

If Arizona State would only offer classes at various times, and were open 24 hours, then he might be able to get himself there successfully at 3 or 4 a.m. Arizona State was not flexible enough to meet that schedule. He needed so much guidance around this, but there was no one to help. Grace, if he had answered his door, would have helped, but she left for the University of Southern California in the fall.

Joe never made it to Arizona State University, and for years, there were only a few knocks on his door. Joe merely existed within the safety of his routines.

# Part VII

*Salamanders are extraordinary survivors and have been on this earth for over 160 million years! Over the last 50 years, over 200 species of amphibians throughout the world have declined markedly in numbers, with reports of 32 species extinctions. In many instances, these declines are attributable to adverse human influences.*

# Chapter One

It had been over fifteen years since Laura had reached out to anyone from her old life. Her new life was exhausting since she was not able to, nor did she want to, live very long at any given location. She followed the news of her friend Shades Creek from afar. They had become friends on Facebook, but only chatted once after their Facebook friendship began. That was about all there was between them for this long period of time. She did enjoy seeing the pictures from the very successful Salamander Festival, and was very proud of Shades, and what he had created, now a Phoenix institution. Every few months she searched for Joe Gamut on Facebook, but after each unsuccessful try, she realized that she would never find him there.

In the years away from Phoenix, Laura had no problem finding work, but mostly her commitment was the issue. She was in a float pool, where she could be assigned temporarily to any Psychiatric Hospital, or to any other hospital unit that needed her. Emotionally, that had become more and more trying. She was in her early fifties now, and at a tipping point where she yearned for the security of being settled. *Isn't that a normal feeling for people entering the "twilight" of their lives?* she thought. Day-to-day, what she was doing wasn't where she'd thought she would end up. Also, the temporary work assignments were becoming more heartbreaking, which increasingly affected her psyche, causing her to crave a drink at home after work, something she could no longer do. She knew that drinking had definitely played a part in her life being unmanageable.

In 2019, Laura had been sober for four years, and during that time, things had gotten better. She'd felt disappointed, looking back at decisions she'd made during times of heavy drinking, but now she viewed them as being in the past. She knew she had to make amends to Joe, but somehow she just couldn't do it. Not acting was justifiable, she thought, because the *Big Book of Alcoholics Anonymous* had taught her that if these amends were to cause someone additional pain, then one should hold off from doing them. Still, it caused her additional pain to think about all that hurt she might have caused Joe. Even when she made amends to herself, she knew she had been a coward.

She also remained single, and mostly celibate, after she stopped drinking. She knew that she had had enough from men in her lifetime, but she also had something to prove to herself: to be a resilient, solid woman, she had to be like, or even better than, her friend Millie had been. Now that the years had gone by, she realized that she had been hard on her friend because she had died. And what were the real reasons for that? She finally let go of her resentment toward Millie— but for Joe, she knew, one day she would have to do something.

\* \* \*

It was the weekend of the Salamader Festival when Laura decided to work through these feelings with her sponsor, a woman with eleven years of sobriety, and twenty-five years her junior.

Laura's sponsor had just grabbed the remote to turn the television off, when a news story was trumpeted by a CNN anchor. The screen's footer read, *CHAOS AT THE SALAMANDER FESTIVAL IN PHOENIX*, and when the video began to roll, Laura jumped up, and the new cross around her neck leapt up and smacked her in the teeth. Laura pointed at the television, while shrieking to her sponsor, "Holy shit! That Salamander is Joe!"

# Chapter Two

About a month before the Salamander Festival, hours past midnight, Joe had been walking to Albertsons. He passed Barney's Costumes, which had elongated its name to a very long: *Barney's Costumes, Official Costume Supplier to The Phoenix Salamander Festival.* Joe stopped every time to look through their display window at the remarkable Superman costume. During the first few years he was alone, Joe would only stop for sentimental reasons, but now it was 2019, and he realized that he had begun to feel a remarkable sense of calm just by staring at it. Joe desperately needed calm. He had successfully divorced himself from the idea of the saving power of Superman after his parents' death, but somehow, today his desperation was all back on the table. It had been years, and his safe routines still gave him no quality of life, and he was still riddled with fear and anxiety. Breathing exercises meant to calm him only caused him to hyperventilate. Counting numbers to 1,000 would only cause him to stand frozen in place. He wondered, if he wore the costume, would things be different this time around? Perhaps the glorious Superman suit was a much more powerful device than a simple terrycloth cape or a cotton tee-shirt. Maybe, he rationalized, those basic articles of protection had only enough power to prevent the small things from happening. Maybe he needed more power for the bigger things.

Each week, when he walked past Barney's before sunrise, these thoughts intensified, and Joe was becoming more and more sold on the idea of becoming a superhero again. Then the grand idea of purchasing the costume rather than having it as a rental came into play. He worried, though: with Laura no longer around, how could he communicate with the store's owner? *What was his name anyway? Barney?*

It was the only logical and quick conclusion he could make.

One early, early, morning, about two weeks before the Salamander Festival, Joe was asked to leave Albertsons when he began to breathe heavily in the cereal aisle. His anxiety, and inability to function in society, had caused him to feel like a total failure. Now, at thirty-six, Joe wished he could succeed in the community without feeling panicked.

On his way home, he walked down Main Street and stopped at the door of Barney's. The store's hours were 10 a.m.–3 p.m., certainly not ideal times for him to avoid people. How would he manage to purchase it? His first plan was to break the glass, but he immediately thought of a probable arrest. Anything could happen if the police were involved. Instead, he broke into a run toward home, and tried to avoid thinking about it. It was ten days of intense planning before he was finally able to leave the house again.

\* \* \*

On the day he felt well enough to go back to Barney's, this time as a customer, the streets of Phoenix were uncomfortably hot, but at least Joe felt he would soon be comfortable within his new skin of the Superman costume. For communication, he had decided that he would scribble a note to the owner, so that he would not have to speak, and it should all be quick and conflict free.

*Dear Barney,* the note read,

*I want to purchase the Superman costume I've seen in your window.*

*I have a debit card.*

*Joe Gamut.*

When he arrived, there was a problem. The Superman costume, for the first time ever, was no longer in the window. It was replaced by a display with five salamander costumes, ready to rent for the festival. He began to shake, but dug his heels into the ground to avoid a full scale blackout. *Maybe it was moved to the back,* he thought. He waited for five minutes, exhaled hard, and walked in. Behind the counter was a gray-bearded man, with a bald, liver-spotted head, that he remembered from years ago.

Shades Creek rubbed his eyes, "Joe?" Then he shouted, "Joe! What can I do for you?"

The question was fairly appropriate, but Joe was surprised, stunned that he had been recognized, especially with such enthusiasm. It wasn't just because of the passing of time. Joe now had hair hung down over his shoulders, which had been cut very unevenly— so how could he have been recognized? He had been 100% reliant on himself for grooming during all these years, as a trip to a barber or hair salon was out of the question. At times, he just shaved his head, but either way, it had been a long time. Joe, because of this turn of events, had a defeated look on his face. He pushed the note to Shades, then shrank back.

"Name's not Barney. It's Shades. Did you forget, Joe?" Joe began breathing more heavily. "And I don't have that suit anymore. In fact, we replaced nearly all the costumes in here with these salamanders. What you want had pretty much hung there forever, and has now been moved to the warehouse." Barney's warehouse was the basement of Shade's house.

Joe looked around. He saw the shop filled 100% with salamander suits.

"Barney's is the official costume supplier and sponsor for the Salamander Festival each year. It's happening next weekend, but you probably knew that."

Joe looked at his feet and counted, *"One one-thousand, two one-thousand, five one-thousand, one million one-thousand."* Counting was always a desperate measure. It never worked. He stood there without movement.

"Ya want one of those salamanders instead? They're all gonna disappear. I sell you one of the older ones, it'll be cheaper. You'll fit right in."

"Yes," Joe responded.

"Okay, great. You still want to buy it?"

"Yes."

"Want to buy a carry bag too?"

"Yes."

Shades zipped the suit into the carry bag as Joe shoved his debit card to him, and the transaction was over. Joe quickly turned, but instead of heading out, he bolted to the dressing room.

"You doing okay?" Shades called after him. "I haven't seen you in quite a while. It's been years."

"Yes," Joe responded, breathing heavily, but knowing he'd only been in the changing room for a few minutes.

\* \* \*

He knew it was just a musty old costume, but Joe decided he'd wear it like a piece of armor—dark green, head-to-foot, furry, with golden spots down the sides—not close at all to Superman, but still, a way to protect him from the world. He thought that no one would stop to talk to him if he wore it, and even if they did, the ridiculous costume would basically eliminate any conflict with another human being or child. He also knew that this high level of fear he experienced lately, causing sweats and shaking, would soon be relieved some.

At home, during the next few days, Joe practiced wearing the suit all the time. *It is only temporary, while the Festival is happening,* he thought, *and until Superman is back in stock.* After a few days, the heavy costume felt comfortable, but it was hot in there, and the large head also bobbled around, bouncing against his, creating vision problems. Three times, he tripped over the coffee table.

*Superhero Salamander,* Joe thought, trying to strengthen the character mentally. *There are going to be many of these guys running around town the next two days, but I'm the one and only Super Sally.* Joe smiled underneath the smelly, heavy shell.

Joe opened the door, and left his house, in the middle of a hot sunny morning, and for the first time in a long time, he did not feel the curtain of anxiety weighing against him. Joe was able to walk through Phoenix, back to Albertsons Market, and in broad daylight. Being a salamander wasn't all that bad, besides the sweating. No one was bothering him. It was close to a perfect setup. He picked Albertsons so he could face, and possibly overcome, a setting which was always uncomfortable for him, especially during normal shopping hours. When he arrived, a few people pointed, while others greeted him enthusiastically. *Oh no,* Joe thought, and everyone seemed to be very excited, and happy.

"On your way to the festival?" they asked.

"Yes, yes," he replied, feeling less protected in his new disguise. At least no one was asking him to do anything. *I should stock up on my food and supplies,* he thought.

He wanted to buy something from every department, but his grandiose ideas pertaining to his new identity, and the urge to snatch and go, which still was present, kept him in produce. Joe purchased a cart full of various types of lettuce, tomatoes, cucumbers, carrots, and corn, as well as some other green leafy vegetables. His cart was piled high, and some spinach fell onto the floor at the register, and the cashier laughed. *This isn't bad at all*, Joe thought. People slapped his back and told him to have fun at the festival. He pushed his cart down West Thomas Road, but then came to a direct halt. He heard someone shout at him.

Joe felt his hair beginning to stand on end, the ones on his back prickling against his salamander suit. He assumed at first that it was Albertsons' manager, and that he was being stopped for removing the shopping cart. It felt eerily familiar, like his first solo effort, "The Incident at Albertsons," half his lifetime ago.

"You!" the man shouted. "Come back here!"

"Yes," Joe said through his muffling garment.

"Come here, we've been waiting for you." The man was standing in front of a white and green family restaurant.

Joe found himself facing an overweight smiling man who wore a white shirt, with a tie, and a nametag which read: *BOB BOULET, MANAGER*, and the restaurant name, *SOUPER SALAD*, centered perfectly under Bob's name and rank. Bob shook Joe's furry hand.

"We've been waiting for you. Here, grab your sign!" It read: *SOUPER SALAD. YOU CAN BE FRESH HERE.* Bob was over-the-top enthusiastic; in fact, he was downright super himself. "Here. Go to the corner and start waving, and flagging down traffic. Remember, The Salamander Festival is one of our busiest promotions here at Souper Salad. We're a sponsor! People want to feel a part of it, so go out there and flag them down."

Joe felt like he was going to pass out.

"And, thanks for the produce!" Bob added, and picked out a tomato from beneath the romaine, taking a bite. "No wonder you're late. I'd been waiting for a truck shipment. Wasn't expecting the shipment to come from the mascot, but this is one hell of a company to work for. You never know what to expect. You know what to do, right?"

"Yes," Joe said. He stood frozen in front of Bob.

"Well, show me," Bob said. "You know... do your act." Bob was obviously excited to see his mascot in action, but Joe wasn't moving. "Okay, fine. Why don't you move to the corner." Joe continued standing in the same spot.

"The street corner! Right there! Move!" Bob shouted.

Under the costume, sweat was running down Joe's forehead, and it stung his eyes. Bob pulled Joe by his green arms. "Flag 'em down, c'mon," Bob said. "Jump around!"

"Yes," Joe said, but when he attempted to jump, a spastic little leap came from his legs, barely propelling him off the ground. Joe's body was now drenched with sweat. Unlike his sign, he smelled very un-fresh.

"Flag 'em down! Flag 'em!" Bob yelled.

Joe knew he had to do something, so he picked up the pace, maniacally jumping at a rapid rate. His furry head moved up and down, jiggling against the top of his real head. He was having zero success directing anyone into the lot, and he looked like he was doing uncoordinated jumping jacks. The Souper Salad sign he held began smashing against the top of the salamander costume head, and the head became more askew on his body. Joe was reminiscent of a hyper bobble-head doll, and the now vibrating head gave the illusion that pressure was building, and that the head would rocket off into space. On top of all that was, through all the movement and fur, Joe could barely hear Bob, who shouted for him to do more and more of something that he couldn't quite understand, nor, at this point, want to do. So, he jumped some more. He jumped in a way that made the head clanging off his cranium, *ba-boom, ba-boom, ba-boom*, completely block the sound of Bob's murky directives. He jumped until he felt tired and dizzy. The heat had got to him, and the earth spun inside the salamander suit. Joe staggered toward the edge of the curb, clipped the edge of it with his bulky feet, and fell head first into West Thomas Street.

\* \* \*

Joe's lack of "social grace" had caused a three-car accident, which caused the death of BOB BOULET, MANAGER, SOUPER SALAD. The entire incident was ruled an accident, but still, Joe was taken by the Arizona Police Department—to be evaluated. In their police report, they wrote:

The first car swerved to avoid the accused's (Joseph Gamut) prone body, and jumped the curb. It came to a stop inches from Bob Boulet. The driver of the third car, also wearing a salamander suit, because he was the real Souper Salad employee, made direct contact with the second car in the line, which careened into the first, pinning Mr. Boulet against the restaurant's wall. The employee, wearing the costume and driving, was cited for sight restricted head ornamentation. The driver (employee) wearing the salamander suit, sustained a head injury when his car door flew open during the impact, and he rolled out of the vehicle, striking his head on the concrete. His safety belt didn't fit over the girth of his suit, so he was not wearing one, and he was also cited for that. This man, in this police officer's opinion, would have died as well, if not for the cushioning of his head, by the costume. Both Mr. Boulet and his employee were taken from the scene by ambulance. Mr. Gamut was taken to Station 151 to be booked and evaluated.

\* \* \*

Joe was brought in by the Phoenix Police in a state of shock and catatonia. There was no evidence of any intentional malice, but because of his current state, Joe ended up being ordered for a complex psychological assessment by the court, and he couldn't answer anything more than a 'yes,' to their questions. Joe was found to be incompetent, and strangely, a danger to himself and others. The evaluator ordered Joe to be kept under care until further notice, so he was moved to a safe, psychiatric setting, with other patients with criminal and social issues, who may or may not have caused fatal traffic accidents. The ward was a tranquil, highly medicated place, so no one bothered him. In fact, there were no demands on him at all. He had few choices to make, but the ones he did, he could handle. After one week, the professionals allowed him to wear a homemade cape around his neck for a few hours, but during the following week, Joe wore his salamander outfit. He, and the professional staff, thought it safer for Joe not to have any conflicts.

# Chapter Three

When Laura arrived, she was taken down a long hallway, and her bag was checked for any dangerous content. "Are you here to see Joe the Salamander? Enjoy talking to him, because he's not saying much," one of the staff workers said, expecting a smile in agreement.

"Um, duh-uh," she said sarcastically, instead.

When she saw Joe seated at the visitors' greeting table in full costume, she threw her arms around him, and started crying. "I'm so sorry, I'm so sorry," she told him. "I just didn't know what to do."

"Yes," Joe said, not able to see who had hugged him, or hear the formerly familiar voice, as the costume did not allow him to see or hear well.

"Miss Wellin," one of the staff yelled. "This is the Criminally Insane Unit. No hugging allowed."

"He's not a fucking criminal, nor is he insane, and I don't know why he is here at all," Laura responded. Joe heard her being called by name, and he hugged her back.

\* \* \*

Laura visited Joe daily, and she stayed at the house at 29 West Sunnyslope Lane. It had been a long time since she'd been there, and it stirred up feelings about the loss of her friend and mentor, Millie. *"They're just feelings, and that's okay,"* she reasoned. *"I should be having feelings. They are normal."* She had no urge to block them out, and every day she called her sponsor.

"How's it going over there? Was the house a complete mess?"

"I'm doing okay, and no, it was impeccably clean. It's weird being in this house, but I'm doing the right thing," Laura responded, caressing the cross around her neck. Steven once swore she would rub the gold clean off if she didn't stop this contemplative habit.

"I'm glad you're sticking with my suggestions," her sponsor added. "Don't try to do too much."

"I'm not. And I've made some progress. I'm praying."

"It's what we do."

"And do you know what?" Laura asked, now pulling the necklace by its chain so it stretched and was taut.

"What?"

"I think things are going to work out. He's on a lot of medication, but if I can get him out of there, I'll definitely have a say about that in the future."

* * *

Laura knew she was strong, and she was like the best strong women who had been present in Joe's life. She was like Grace, and she was like Millie. They were like pit bulls when it came to advocacy, and producing results for Joe. Joe hadn't had someone like Laura in his life since his mother died and Grace left for college. Laura was making amends to Joe of the best kind: life changing amends.

To begin with, it was obvious to Laura that Joe was not guilty of anything, nor was he insane, which in legal terms meant he had no idea or grasp of reality, of what was going on, at the time it was happening. The court psychiatrist, with only Joe present, was not able to get an objective assessment of Joe, nor was there even one other opinion on the overall mental health and stability of Joe Gamut. Legally, since he'd been placed in a ward for the criminally insane, getting him out, even with all of her psychiatric nursing expertise, would be a challenge, but it was a goal Laura knew was achievable.

Laura gathered up all Joe's records from high school, and even Dr. Ogden's old evaluation from way back, to form an appeal for another court date. She even consulted with two lawyers. One was her divorce lawyer, and the other was the Gamuts' family lawyer; neither of them was a criminal lawyer, but both were able to give their opinion. The divorce lawyer suggested highly that Joe get a haircut and clean up a bit. The Gamuts' lawyer remained consistent in his opinion, just as he had been to Richard and Samantha, that Joe would be okay out in the community. For a fee, which Joe would pay him later, he submitted a letter on behalf of Joe. It began:

*Ladies and Gentleman of the court, I have known Joseph Gamut and his entire family, most of his life....*

# Chapter Four

The first thing that Joe wanted to do when he arrived back home
was to take an hour for decompression in his room. He wanted to
sit there alone, listening to music, so he could adapt to his new/old
bearings and think about what he needed to change in order to have
success. He had been released by the court, under the care of Laura,
who agreed during the hearing that she would move in, and of course,
Joe agreed as well, answering 'yes,' to the judge the same definitive
way he had answered during the course of his lifetime. It was then,
when he was all cleaned up, wearing a suit and with a fresh haircut,
that Laura saw how handsome a man he was. Laura felt suddenly
vulnerable, her nerves dancing in her stomach, like a million beautiful
butterflies.

\* \* \*

Laura did not allow him to wear the salamander suit on the way
home, not even the head, which Joe had attempted to slip on.

"No," Laura said. "Those things got you in a lot of trouble. We
need to avoid trouble. You're kind of on probation here. I'm going
to be in charge, so just do what I say, kind of like a sponsor."

"Yes," Joe said.

"Oh, you don't really understand what a sponsor does...."

"Yes," Joe said.

"No matter. Just stick with my suggestions, and you'll see your
life improving. It will keep things good, and right... the way they
were when your mother was alive."

Joe knew how his mother used to do things, and he knew that
part of the reason for this success was because he could speak to her,

so that things could be explained better. His mother also pushed him past his comfort zones in ways no one else could. He didn't want to be in any more trouble, because he needed his life to be more manageable. He was glad Laura was here. She was familiar, and he trusted her. He had had enough desperation about his life to recently try the same old things which hadn't worked, which led to his being locked in an institution. That was pretty much his bottom. It took him the hour in his room to determine he was ready to try something new.

In that hour, he concluded that Laura represented all of the things that had soothed him all his life. She was the stones he used to sit on, the shows and movies he used to watch, the music he listened to, the books he read, the parents that he lost, and she was the only person left who had loved him his entire life.

After an hour, Joe walked out of his room and stood in front of Laura. It was an old and odd behavior which she smiled at. She remembered that this is what Joe did when she lived there the six months after her divorce. If it were anyone else, it still would have been creepy, but with Joe, it always felt like a compliment.

"Oh, so I see how it is," she said, chuckling at the clever tone she was using, and the flirtatiousness of the message. "Are you here to thank me, handsome man, or do you still have that little crush on me that you used to?" She waited for his 'yes,' but the response came out a little hoarse, and at a low volume—yet the weight of it was as bold, and as loud as a public address system. It knocked the silly grin off of Laura's face, and physically caused her to stumble back a few steps. "Thank you, Laura," was the response, "And, yes."

# Chapter Five

Laura had decorated both the inside and the outside of the house at 29 West Sunnyslope Lane. Only a few guests attended, because at this point in their lives, they didn't really know too many people whom they actually could invite. Joe would have been nervous around a group larger than ten anyway. Shades Creek was invited as long as he wore nothing having to do with the Salamander Festival, or salamanders in general—especially not a salamander suit. Laura also had to make sure Shades had no resentments toward Joe for the "bad publicity" he'd brought to the festival. Shades Creek did not, and he happily attended. Laura's parents were invited, as were Joe's grandparents, but neither the bride nor groom much wanted either of them there. They were more there for decoration, like the four plastic cacti Laura had brought into the living room. There were more than enough pricks in the house, so what's a few more, Laura had joked.

Joe wore a tuxedo, and Laura again wore white, which was the symbol for joy, rather than virginity. Her sponsor gave her away, rather than her father. The minister approved of Joe saying, 'yes,' instead of 'I do,' but was never given the reason. Laura confided in Joe that it didn't matter to her, and it was, "None of the minister's damned business."

Joe and Laura lived their life together quietly, and without much stress. Laura taught Joe that when he thought about Superman all these years, he was really thinking about God, and He, like Superman, was not to be blamed when bad things happened. And when Joe thought about salamanders, he thought that there are more than 400 known salamander species still in existence, including newts, and although some characteristics are shared by many, some species are completely unique——and that was completely okay.

CPSIA information can be obtained
at www.ICGtesting.com
Printed in the USA
BVHW081401120722
641843BV00025B/726

9 781952 232695